Education and Internally Displaced Persons

Also available in the Education as a Humanitarian Response Series

Education as a Global Concern, Colin Brock
Education and HIV/AIDS, Nalini Asha Biggs
Education and Reconciliation, Julia Paulson
Education and Minorities, Chris Atkin
Education, Aid and Aid Agencies, Zuki Karpinska
Education, Refugees and Asylum Seekers, Lala Demirdjian

Education and Internally Displaced Persons

Education as Humanitarian Response

Edited by

Christine Smith Ellison and Alan Smith

BLOOMSBURY

LONDON • NEW DELHI • NEW YORK • SYDNEY

Bloomsbury Academic
An imprint of Bloomsbury Publishing Plc

50 Bedford Square   175 Fifth Avenue
London   New York
WC1B 3DP   NY 10010
UK   USA

www.bloomsbury.com

First published 2013

British Library Cataloguing-in-Publication Data
A catalogue record for this book is available from the British Library.

ISBN: HB: 978-1-4411-7214-3
      PB: 978-1-4411-9649-1
      PDF: 978-1-4411-9047-5
      ePub: 978-1-4411-0613-1

Library of Congress Cataloging-in-Publication Data
A catalog record for this book is available from the Library of Congress.

Typeset by Fakenham Prepress Solutions, Fakenham, Norfolk NR21 8NN
Printed and bound in Great Britain

Contents

Notes on Contributors

Christine Smith Ellison is a Research Associate in Education, Conflict and International Development at the UNESCO Centre, University of Ulster, UK. Her work entails examining the linkages between education, conflict and the UN peacebuilding agenda, and undertaking political economy analysis of the education sector. She holds an MA (Hons) in Anthropology and French from the University of Glasgow, UK, and an MPhil in International Development from the University of Oxford, UK.

Anne Lauten currently works as the Norwegian Refugee Council's Gender Based Violence Project Manager in Liberia. Anne specializes in protection and child protection programming in emergencies, having worked with the International Rescue Committee in Chad and the Central African Republic and the Watchlist on Children and Armed Conflict in Nepal, Democratic Republic of Congo, Colombia and Sudan prior to joining the NRC. Anne has supported academic research on the protective impact of education for children in Nepal, post-tsunami Aceh, Indonesia, and post-Katrina New Orleans, USA.

Silje Sjøvaag Skeie is Education advisor for the Norwegian Refugee Council (NRC), where she provides technical support to NRC's education programs for conflict-affected children and youth in Africa. Prior to that, Silje managed NRC's education programme in Somalia. She is a member of the Inter-Agency Network for Education in Emergencies (INEE) and the Inter-Agency Standing Committee (IASC) Education Cluster Working Group. Previously, Silje worked for UNESCO and various NGOs in Africa and Asia.

Kevin Watkins is a Senior Fellow with the Center for Universal Education at Brookings, USA, and a Senior Visiting Research Fellow at University College, University of Oxford, UK. Previously, he was the director and lead author of UNESCO's Education For All Global Monitoring Report after serving for three years as the director of the UNDP Human Development Report, where he led the research on reports covering the Millennium Development Goals, water and climate change. Prior to working with the United Nations, he worked for thirteen years with Oxfam, where he authored major reports on African debt, international trade and Oxfam's Education Report.

Manuel José Cepeda-Espinosa is Director of the Programme on Public Policies at the Law School, Universidad de los Andes, Bogotá, Colombia. In his positions as Justice and President of the Constitutional Court he was responsible for decision T-025 of 2004 granting protection to Colombian IDPs. Previous positions include Dean of the Law School at the Universidad de los Andes, Colombia, Ambassador of Colombia to UNESCO, and thereafter to the Helvetic Confederation. As Presidential Advisor to both César Gaviria Trujillo (1990–1) and Virgilio Barco Vargas (1987–90) he promoted the creation of a Constituent Assembly, the drafting of the 1991 Colombian Constitution and several statutes to protect fundamental rights such as *tutela* and the rules of the Constitutional Court.

Elizabeth Ferris is Senior Fellow in Foreign Policy and Co-Director of the Brookings-LSE Project on Internal Displacement in Washington, DC, USA, where her work encompasses a wide range of issues related to forced migration, human rights, humanitarian action, the role of civil society in protecting displaced populations and the security implications of displacement. Prior to joining Brookings in November 2006, she spent 20 years working in the field of humanitarian assistance, most recently in Geneva, Switzerland at the World Council of Churches, where she was responsible for the Council's work in humanitarian response and long-term development.

Chareen Stark is a Senior Research Assistant at the Brookings-LSE Project on Internal Displacement in Washington, DC, USA Prior to joining Brookings in January 2009, she worked with the United Nations Development Programme (UNDP) and the United Nations Relief and Works Agency (UNRWA) in Jerusalem, Israel.

Lynn Davies is Emeritus Professor of International Education at the University of Birmingham, UK. She has published major books and reports, including *Education and Conflict: Complexity and Chaos* (which won the Society of Education Studies prize for the best book of 2004); *Educating Against Extremism* (2008); and *Capacity Development for Education Systems in Fragile Contexts* (2009: ETF/GTZ/INEE). Research grants have included awards for work in education and vulnerabilities in emergencies in South Asia (UNICEF); the impact of school councils (Esmee Fairburn/Deutsche Bank); education for peace and social cohesion in Sri Lanka (GIZ); primary education in post-conflict Angola (cfBT); democratic education in the Gambia (Cfbt); and global citizenship education (DFID).

Valery Perry first worked in Bosnia and Herzegovina (BiH) in 1997 as an election supervisor. She has lived in Sarajevo since 1999, conducting research and working for organizations including the NATO Stabilization Force (SFOR), the European Center for Minority Issues (ECMI) and several NGOs. She worked at the OSCE Mission to Bosnia and Herzegovina in Sarajevo from 2004–11 as Deputy Director of the Education Department, and Deputy Director of the Human Dimension Department. She currently works as Chief of Party for the Public International Law and Policy Group (PILPG) in Sarajevo, implementing a project to increase civil society engagement in constitutional reform processes in Bosnia and Herzegovina.

Marina Bowder first came to Bosnia and Herzegovina in 1995, the last year of the conflict, and has lived there ever since. Her first professional post was with Sarajevo University, Bosnia and Herzegovina, but she also worked extensively for the Office of the High Representative (OHR) on issues obstructing refugee return, including education. She subsequently moved to the Organization for Security and Co-operation in Europe, where she became Head of Section for Diversity and Inclusion in Schools. She has now returned to the English Department of Sarajevo University and also teaches in a local school. She holds an MA from Trinity College, Cambridge, UK.

Alan Smith is the UNESCO Chair in Education at the University of Ulster, UK. He has worked closely with education authorities during the conflict and as part of the peace process in Northern Ireland and has completed assignments for DFID, GTZ, International Alert, Save the Children, UNESCO, UNICEF and the World Bank in the Basque Country, Bosnia, Serbia, Sierra Leone, Sri Lanka, Nepal, Nigeria and Zimbabwe. He was an adviser to the Education for All, Global Monitoring Report (2011) on education and armed conflict and is currently involved in a UNICEF global study on the role of education in peacebuilding.

Series Editor's Preface

Underlying this entire series on *Education as a Humanitarian Response* is the well-known adage in education that 'if we get it right for those most in need we will likely get it right for all if we take the same approach.' That sentiment was born in relation to those with special educational needs within a full mainstream system of schooling. In relation to this series it is taken further to embrace not only the special educational needs of those experiencing disasters and their aftermath, whether natural or man-made, but also to other groups who may be significantly disadvantaged. Indeed, much can be learned of value to the provision of mainstream systems from the holistic approach that necessarily follows in response to situations of disaster. Sadly very little of this potential value is actually perceived, and even less is embraced. Consequently one of the aims of the series, both in the core volume *Education as a Global Concern* and the contributing volumes, is to bring to the mainstream, and to those seeking to serve it as teachers, other educators and politicians, the notion of education as a humanitarian response.

The situation of Internally Displaced Peoples is one in which this issue is most strikingly illustrated in terms of the disconnect between education in emergencies and education for sustainable development. The starkness of the separation is highlighted by the fact of it being within one country. It is further compounded by the additional difficulty experienced by external and internal agencies seeking to help as compared with assisting refugees, though this is not necessarily the case with regard to displacement due to natural disasters. The number of IDPs in the world considerably outnumbers that of refugees, yet the difficulties of external access mean that we know much less about IDPs, their educational needs and the responses to those needs. Consequently, the global overview provided in this volume, plus the case studies from widely differing locations and environments, make a distinctive and valuable contribution to the growing literature of education as a humanitarian response.

Colin Brock
UNESCO Chair in Education as
a Humanitarian Response, University of Oxford, UK.

Introduction: A Global Overview of Education and IDPs

Christine Smith Ellison

Chapter Outline

Key Facts

Global Number	27 million
Key Document	1998 Guiding Principles
Primary Responsibility	National government
Monitoring Body	Norwegian Refugee Council's Internal Displacement Monitoring Centre (IDMC)
Most affected region	Africa (11.1 million IDPs in 21 countries)
Number of countries with people living in protracted displacement	At least 40
Durable Solutions	Return
	Local Integration
	Settlement elsewhere
Number of internally displaced children	At least 13.5 million

(IDMC 2011a; Ferris and Winthrop 2010)

The recent Global Monitoring Report 2011 focused on 'the hidden crisis: armed conflict and education', and highlighted the alarming fact that 42% of the world's out-of school children live in conflict-affected states. As the nature of conflict changes and wars are fought within rather than between states, an increasing number of children are displaced from their homes and lack access to education. This chapter provides an overview of internal displacement presenting key trends in the patterns of displacement, the arguments as to why IDPs are a category of concern and the options for durable solutions. The chapter then examines the specific challenges for education, including the legislative support for the right to education, the barriers faced by IDPs in accessing this right and current national and international responses.

Displacement

Refugees and IDPs: the differences

> A refugee is defined as a person who, 'owing to a well-founded fear of being persecuted for reasons of race, religion, nationality, memberships of a particular group or political opinion, is outside the country of his nationality and is unable or, owing to such fear, is unwilling to avail himself of the protection of that country'.
>
> 1951 Convention Relating to the Status of Refugees, Art. 1 A.2

> IDPs are 'persons or groups of persons who have been forced or obliged to flee or to leave their homes or places of habitual residence, in particular as a result of or in order to avoid the effects of armed conflict, situations of generalized violence, violations of human rights or natural or human-made disasters and who have not crossed an internationally recognized State border'.
>
> 1998 Guiding Principles on Internal Displacement

It is sometimes mistakenly believed that internally displaced persons are simply 'refugees' who have not crossed an internationally recognized border. Both groups can at times share similar experiences including the trauma of displacement, separation from family and support networks, and often discrimination and poverty in their place of relocation. At different stages of disaster individuals can even be both, for example, those displaced by conflict in Darfur move between eastern Chad and the Sudan depending on the level of security threat (UNESCO, 2011: 154). However, there are three important differences between the two groups which can have significant consequences for responses.

First, there are differences in how refugees and IDPs are defined in relation to international law. Refugees are covered by a legal framework provided by the 1951 UN Convention relating to the Status of Refugees and its 1967 Protocol. There are now 144 States Parties to the Convention and 147 States Parties to one or both instruments (Ferris and Winthrop 2010: 6). This framework includes internationally accepted norms, rights and entitlements for refugees and a UN agency (UNHCR) with a mandate to enforce them (UNESCO, 2011).

In contrast, there is no legally binding instrument upholding the specific rights of internally displaced persons. Rather, the Guiding Principles on Internal Displacement were presented to the UN in 1998 and endorsed by the General Assembly in the 2005 World Summit Outcome document. They are consistent with existing international human rights law and international humanitarian law and restate in greater detail existing guarantees that apply particularly to IDPs. However, the Guiding Principles are not an international convention or treaty or legally binding instrument.

The second distinction relates to the causes of displacement: the conditions leading to internal displacement are much broader. Exactly how far the definition should extend has been the subject of much discussion, with some debating whether those displaced by development projects and even economic migrants in the context of extreme poverty should be considered IDPs (Mooney, 2005). Others argue that the definition is too broad as it stands and in a similar way to the refugee definition, should be limited to those displaced due to conflict or persecution (Castles et al., 2005). However, the definition included in the Guiding Principles clearly extends beyond those forced to flee due to conflict and persecution to include those displaced due to natural and human-made disaster. This is because it is considered that these individuals share distinct protection and assistance needs arising from the involuntary nature of their movement. The great variety of circumstances faced by IDPs calls for creativity and a strong knowledge base on which to base humanitarian responses.

Finally, internal displacement refers to movement within national borders. This may seem like an obvious point, but it has important implications for the level of protection and assistance that an IDP may receive. International law upholds the concept of national sovereignty. As discussed, the IDP definition is a descriptive one and does not confer a special legal status in the same way that recognition as a refugee does. This is because 'the rights and guarantees to which IDPs are entitled stem from the fact that they are human beings and citizens or habitual residents of a particular state' (Walter Kalin quoted in Mooney 2005). The protection of IDPs is the responsibility of the national government. However, this is clearly problematic when it is the national government that is the agent of displacement as was the case in almost half the internal displacement situations monitored by the Internal Displacement Monitoring Centre (IDMC) in 2010 (IDMC, 2011a: 10). It may also be the case that the capacity of the government is destroyed due to the crisis that has caused displacement. In this case the international community has a duty to ensure that the rights of IDPs are maintained. However, access must ultimately be granted by national governments, and cases where this access has been denied or limited demonstrate the complexities of the humanitarian space.

Patterns of displacement

Global statistics reinforce the misconception that internal displacement refers only to persons uprooted by conflict, violence and persecution. While the Internal Displacement Monitoring Centre (IDMC) has monitored internal displacement resulting from conflict and violence since 1998, the first global estimate of natural disaster-induced displacement was produced in 2009. The two data sets are collected separately and presented yearly in two separate reports. All figures should be treated with caution and understood within the context of the following provisos. The statistics collected on natural disaster-induced displacement are important to mention as they indicate the scale of displacement and the variability from year to year. However, the figures collected refer to all people displaced by natural disasters. While the report indicates that 'globally, the large majority of people displaced by disasters caused by sudden-onset hazards remain internally displaced', it does not distinguish between those who have been internally displaced within their country and those who have crossed an international border (IDMC, 2011b). Furthermore, both sets of data almost certainly under-represent the problem. Reporting systems are extremely restricted and in some cases, such as Angola and Sierra Leone, governments simply decided that there are no longer IDPs, even though many of those displaced have yet to find durable solutions (Ferris and Winthrop, 2010: 3).

In some cases the statistics simply raise more questions. Statistics collected in the context of conflict include reference to those living in protracted displacement. However, there is no information on the finding of durable solutions. On the other hand, statistics relating to natural disaster-induced displacement refer only to the number of newly displaced persons each year and therefore do not give any indication of length of displacement. The methodology used for data collection also focuses on new displacement, triggered by '*sudden-onset* disasters' (IDMC, 2011b). This means it includes geophysical events, such as volcanic eruptions, earthquakes and tsunamis, and climate-related events such as floods, storms, extreme temperatures and wildfires. However, it also means there are other forms of displacement that it does not take into account. In particular, the challenges facing those forced to flee due to slow-onset disasters such as drought require attention.

Conflict-induced Displacement: the figures

Displacement is a primary consequence of conflict. According to a survey by the International Committee of the Red Cross, 56% of people affected by conflict have been displaced. In some cases the proportion affected is even higher: over the course of their conflicts 76% of the population in Afghanistan and 90% of Liberians were forced to flee (ICRC, 2009: 6). Ferris and Winthrop (2010: 5) identify three ways in which conflict leads to displacement. First, civilians can be 'caught in the crossfire' and either flee once violence reaches their community or flee in anticipation of conflict. Secondly, armed groups may adopt an explicit strategy aimed at causing displacement of specific individuals or groups of individuals. At other times they may seek to create widespread displacement. Thirdly, displacement results from the disruption of economic and social life brought about by conflict.

Since 1998 the Internal Displacement Monitoring Centre (IDMC) has monitored internal displacement resulting from armed conflict, generalized violence and human rights violations. According to its most recent report, as of December 2010 approximately 27.5 million were internally displaced worldwide (IDMC, 2011a). The changing nature of contemporary conflict which sees an increasing number of wars being fought within rather than between borders appears to be having an impact on patterns of displacement. While there has been a longer-term upward trend in the number of IDPs,

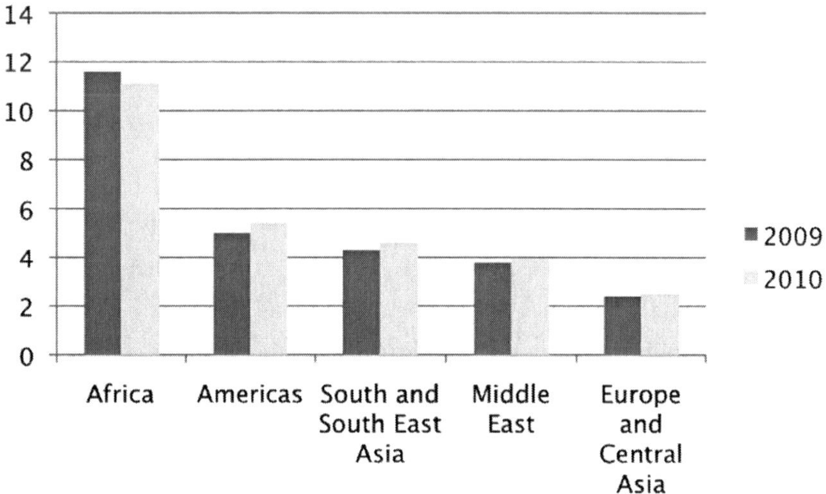

Figure 1 IDP Estimates by Region (millions of people)
Data source IDMC 2011a

from around 17 million in 1997, the number of refugees has remained fairly stable, fluctuating between 13 million and 16 million.

The report indicates that the largest number of IDPs is overwhelmingly in Africa, where there were 11.1 million IDPs at the end of 2010. That is more than twice as many as in the Americas, the region with the second highest number at 5.4 million. However, Africa is also the only region which experienced an overall decrease in the number of IDPs in 2010.

Natural Disaster-induced Displacement: the figures

The first global estimate of the scale of this form of displacement was produced in 2009 by the IDMC and the UN's Office for the Coordination of Humanitarian Affairs (OCHA). According to the latest report over 42 million people were displaced due to disasters triggered by sudden-onset natural disasters in 2010 (IDMC, 2011b). It is already apparent from the figures collected that there is great variability in the numbers displaced due to natural disasters from year to year. Climate-related disasters, primarily floods and storms, are the main cause of displacement. They were responsible for the displacement of over 15 million people in 2009 and over 38 million people in 2010. Displacement triggered by geophysical disasters, volcanic eruptions, earthquakes and tsunamis, was also significant, with at least 1.5 million uprooted in 2009 and over four million in 2010. The huge numbers

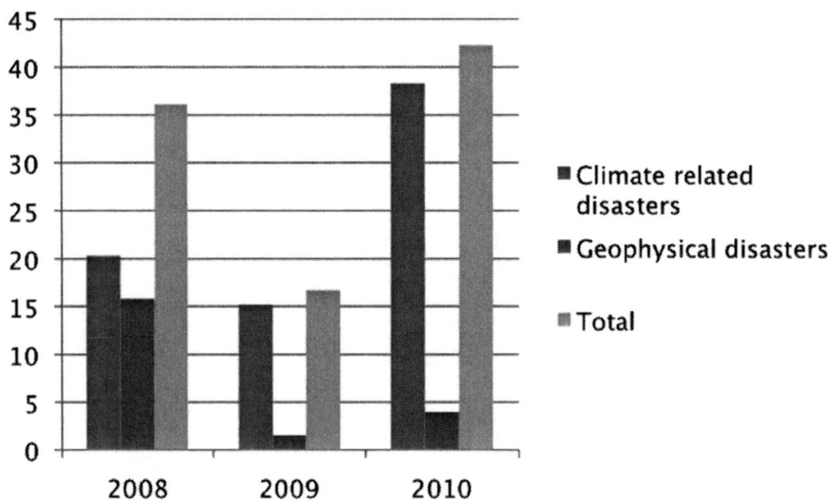

Figure 2 Numbers of Displaced (millions of people)
Data Source IDMC 2010b

and variations between years are largely due to the impact of the large-scale disasters. Between 2008 and 2010, 86 disasters displaced 100,000 or more people, including 18 'mega-disasters' which each displaced from one million (2008 Sichaun earthquake) to over 15 million (2010 floods in China).

The scale of movement and issues involved in the two types of displacement clearly differ, and each set of circumstances requires a separate and relevant response. However, it is possible to identify two trends in the pattern of internal displacement that have important implications for humanitarian, and in particular educational, planning. The first relates to duration. While IDP situations are often characterized by a great deal of fluidity and change, many IDPs are displaced for long periods of time. In 2010 the IDMC identified situations of protracted displacement in around 40 countries (IDMC 2011a: 28), including Colombia, Georgia, Sri Lanka and Uganda (Ferris and Winthrop, 2010: 9). In terms of planning it is vital that all responses are forward-looking: many of the challenges of protracted displacement arise as individuals spend years living and being educated in what were originally designed as temporary arrangements. Furthermore, as many of the chapters in this book demonstrate, what appears as protracted displacement may in reality be a series of displacements as individuals are forced from one form of temporary shelter to the next. Serious thought needs to be given to the flexibility of responses, with particular attention paid to the issue of certification to ensure students may enrol in education without having to repeat prior learning.

The second trend relates to location. While the common perception is of displaced persons living in camps, the IDMC reports that 'the majority of IDPs in the world lived outside gathered settings' (2011a: 13), often fleeing to cities in the search for economic activity. Life in displacement camps presents its own challenges including 'lack of security, increased levels of domestic and community violence, sexual exploitation and abuse, and dependency on international assistance' (Ferris and Winthrop, 2010: 9). However, those outside camps can often be invisible to humanitarian actors and agencies and, in this respect, could be considered more vulnerable. There are a number of challenges to providing protection and assistance to urban IDPs. On a practical level it can be very difficult to identify IDPs widely dispersed in urban locations. This is exacerbated by a lack of registration and information. Moreover, urban IDPs may actively seek invisibility for security reasons (Montemurro and Walicki, 2010). IDPs fleeing to the city also tend to find shelter in poorer parts of the city where non-IDPs face many of the same hardships related to poverty. This leads to concern over singling out IDPs with targeted interventions which can lead to hostility and friction between IDPs and their 'host' community. In this case more integrated approaches targeted at both populations may be more effective. However, it must also be recognised that many urban IDPs will have specific needs related to their displacement, including assistance with return as well as compensation for loss of property.

Conditions Faced by IDPs

While it is difficult to generalize about the conditions facing IDPs, they do have certain needs arising from their displacement which render them vulnerable. Most obviously, the fact of having to flee means that IDPs are forced to leave their home and are therefore deprived of shelter and the basic protection it provides. This can be particularly traumatic for indigenous or pastoralist groups with a strong attachment to land. For example, in 2010 this occurred in Afghanistan, Colombia, Ethiopia, Kenya and Somalia (IDMC, 2011a: 9).

The flight itself is often dangerous and, added to the experiences that many will have undergone before fleeing, many IDPs suffer from physical and psychological trauma. Family members often become separated and the loss of support networks can heighten vulnerability in displacement. Furthermore, the threat of insecurity does not always end in displacement. There are many examples of heightened gender-based violence in displacement camps (Okello and Hovil 2007). There are also instances of the militarization of IDP camps. For example, in 2010 the security of IDPs in camps in Darfur was compromised by the availability of small arms. 'Clashes in Kalma camp in July resulted in the death of four people and injuries to seven others. The security situation within the camp deteriorated further, as shooting and conflict led to at least 35 fatalities and the secondary displacement of 25,000 IDPs from the camp to surrounding areas' (IDMC 2011a: 25). Similarly, fleeing to urban areas does not necessarily lead to safety. In Somalia, for example, 'thousands of IDPs in the town of Beletweyne were repeatedly forced to flee by fighting between rival armed groups. Heavy shelling of the town's central area forced 35,000 to 40,000 IDPs to flee to other areas' (IDMC 2011a: 25). Further complication arises from the fact that whilst the responsibility to protect IDPs lies with national governments, they are often the reason for displacement: in 2010 in almost half of all internal situations monitored by the IDMC, the agents of displacement were government forces or armed groups allied with them (IDMC 2011a: 14). The insecurity which IDPs face also reduces the chance that humanitarian assistance will reach them.

Unable to make use of their land and traditional livelihoods, it can be difficult for IDPs to find a means of income. They may be obliged to settle in isolated or economically marginal areas where land is poor or where the potential for formal or informal employment is restricted. This means that one of the most urgent needs is food; IDPs typically comprise the majority of beneficiaries of World Food Programme assistance (Mooney, 2005: 16). Moreover, IDPs heightened levels of food and insecurity do not necessarily improve over time. Mooney quotes a study by the ICRC and WFP in Colombia which 'found no indication that households who have been displaced for a long time have the ability to generate the income needed to obtain sufficient food (Mooney, 2005: 16). This can lead to a reliance on humanitarian assistance and the development of a 'culture of dependency'.

IDPs are often displaced into areas where they are a minority. This can lead to tension and hostility from hosts who may resent the strain on their already limited resources. Resentments can be exacerbated by the targeting of IDPs for assistance in a context where hosts are often among the most marginalized segments of their own community. This leaves IDPs open to discrimination and stigmatization. This can be made worse by policies and practices which fail to consider their distinct needs and so put them at a disadvantage. For example, 'for 15 years the government of Georgia focused on the return of IDPs and therefore had no policy to ensure appropriate accommodation. Since 2009 while the government has recognised the need to improve living conditions of IDPs, the improvements have taken place for IDPs living in government-owned collective centres and not yet for IDPs in private accommodation. Some of these IDPs have reported discrimination in accessing adequate housing as landlords viewed them as a risky category of rent payers' (IDMC, 2011a: 23).

It is also common for IDPs to lack identity documents. They may have been lost in flight or destroyed in the course of violence or as a result of natural disaster. In Sri Lanka it is estimated that more than 70% of survivors of the tsunami of December 2004 lost their documentation (Mooney, 2005: 17). In some cases displaced persons, fearing persecution, may have destroyed the documents themselves. This can inhibit their access to health care, education and other social services and can make resolving land issues extremely difficult. As voting rights are tied to place of residence, a lack of documentation may also leave IDPs unable to exercise their right to have say in the decisions that affect their lives.

Women and children face particular abuses and challenges during displacement. Sexual and gender-based violence is one of the most pervasive violations of the rights of women and girls during armed conflict and displacement (IDMC, 2011a). Internally displaced children are especially vulnerable to recruitment by armed forces. In 2010 the IDMC reported that 'IDP camps and informal settlements continued to be prime recruiting grounds, as children there were relatively densely gathered, often without access to education (particularly those of secondary-level age) and unable to engage in other livelihood activities' (IDMC, 2011a: 24). In fact women and children tend to suffer disproportionately from the challenges affecting all IDPs. Often the target of discrimination, women heading internally displaced households face obstacles in finding income-generating activities with which to support their families. In the context of poverty it is often women and children who are forced to engage in economic activities that threaten their security. Furthermore, it is women and children who, finding themselves widowed, orphaned or separated from their family, are unlikely to have documentation in their own names.

Durable Solutions

Principle 6 of the Guiding Principles states that 'displacement shall last no longer than required by the circumstances' and the right of IDPs to a durable solution is articulated in Principles 28–30. As the Guiding Principles do not contain the equivalent of the cessation clause in refugee law, the international community has recently developed indicators to help in determining when internal displacement ends. Endorsed by the Inter-Agency Standing Committee in December 2009, the revised Framework on Durable Solutions for Internally Displaced Persons establishes that a durable solution is achieved when 'IDPs no longer have specific assistance and protection needs that are linked to their displacement, and can enjoy their human rights without discrimination on account of their displacement' (IASC, 2010: 5).

The Framework identifies three settlement options that should be available to IDPs: sustainable reintegration at the place of origin (return); sustainable local integration in areas where IDPs have taken refuge (local integration); or sustainable integration in another part of the country (settlement elsewhere). It also identifies eight criteria which should be used when considering whether a durable solution has been achieved:

- Long-term safety, security and freedom of movement
- An adequate standard of living, including at a minimum access to adequate food, water, housing, health care and basic education
- Access to employment and livelihoods
- Access to effective mechanisms that restore their housing, land and property or provide them with compensation
- Access to and replacement of personal and other documentation
- Voluntary reunification with family members separated during displacement
- Participation in public affairs at all levels on an equal basis with the resident population
- Effective remedies for displacement-related violations, including access to justice, reparations and information about the causes of violations.

According to the Guiding Principles it is the duty of national authorities to ensure that the conditions are in place for IDPs to achieve a durable solution to their displacement. It is also their responsibility to ensure that IDPs have the information they need to make a voluntary choice between the three settlement options. However, in practice governments often have a bias towards return. For example, while Uganda's IDP policy acknowledges the three options, their practice has been to promote return, with some politicians seeking to highlight camp closures, 'homecomings' and the 'normalization' of the situation for political gain (IDMC, 2011a: 28).

Other governments, faced with the reality that return may not currently be possible, have made progress towards supporting local integration as a settlement option. For more than fifteen years Georgia had no policy to ensure decent housing for IDPs as its focus was on return. However, following the war with Russia in 2008 and a second wave of displacement, the government has started to invest in improving current living conditions by gradually renovating collective centres and passing the ownership of spaces in some cases to IDPs (IDMC, 2011a: 29).

Despite these developments, many IDPs live with 'no solutions in sight' (Crisp, 2002). In 2010 the IDMC identified situations of protracted displacement in around 40 countries (IDMC, 2011a: 28), including Colombia, Georgia, Sri Lanka and Uganda (Ferris and Winthrop 2010: 9). There is recognition that there is a need to move beyond traditional approaches to assistance and the three solutions framework. However more research is needed into what this may look like in practice. Recent research into situations of protracted displacement identified the 'fundamental cause' as 'a crisis of citizenship or governance in a community or state of origin. This may result from an absence or an excess of state authority' (Long, 2011: 37). It highlights the links that exist between emergency and protracted situations: 'protracted displacement is often a result of continued cycles of displacement that follow new iterations of crisis and are thus dynamic and constantly changing, not stagnant or static' (Long, 2011: 37). The study concludes that discussions 'must be framed by broader peacebuilding and state-building discourses, and that final resolution of protracted displacement is contingent on the (re)building of viable state governance structures' (2011: 37). It calls for development, security and political actors, including IDPs, to be involved in establishing frameworks for 'solutions'.

The Right to Education in Displacement

Right to Education

> 'Everyone has the right to education. Education shall be free, at least in the elementary and fundamental phases. Elementary education shall be compulsory'
> Universal Declaration of Human Rights Article 26

> 'Every human being has the right to education'
> Guiding Principles on Internal Displacement 23(1)

The right to education has been recognized since the Universal Declaration of Human Rights in 1948. It has been enshrined in a number of human rights treaties including the Convention on Economic, Social and Cultural Rights (ICESCR, 1966), the Convention on Elimination of All Forms of Racial Discrimination, the Convention on Elimination of Discrimination Against Women (CEDAW, 1979) and the Convention on the Rights of the Child (CRC, 1989). It has also been incorporated into a number of regional treaties including the African Charter of Human and Peoples' Rights and the European Convention on Human Rights.

The Guiding Principles reiterate that all people have the right to education, including those who are internally displaced. Guiding Principle 23 stresses that education 'shall be made available to internally displaced people, in particular adolescents and women, whether or not living in camps, as soon as conditions permit'. It states that primary education must be free and compulsory. The right to education in displacement also extends to general 'education programmes' and 'training'. It is not limited to the period of displacement but applies also in the contexts of durable solutions, as specified in Guiding Principle 29 (1).

In 1999 the UN Committee on Economic, Social and Cultural Rights outlined four essential elements of the right to education: availability, accessibility, acceptability and adaptability (the 'Four As'). As outlined in the IDMC Briefing Paper, *Learning in Displacement* (2010), certain aspects of the four As framework take on particular importance in the context of internal displacement:

Availability

Free and compulsory primary education should be available for all. In the context of displacement this means schools should be available to all IDPS, whether living in camps or elsewhere. Alternative facilities may be appropriate for short-term periods in displacement settings. Economic costs should not act as a barrier to attending school. Measures should be taken to ensure adequate infrastructure and trained teachers able to support education delivery.

Accessibility

Education provision must be non-discriminatory and accessible to all. Internally displaced children must be able to reach educational services without the risk of attack. Discrimination against IDPs or within the IDP population against minorities, girls and other groups is prohibited. Positive steps should be taken to include the most marginalized.

Acceptability

Education content should be relevant, non-discriminatory and culturally appropriate. 'The notion of respect for cultural identity and language is especially relevant for displaced children from minority backgrounds, who may find themselves in areas dominated by different ethnic groups' (IDMC, 2010: 6).

Adaptability

Education must be flexible and respond to the best interest of each child. Displacement can last for many years: education should help children adapt to their current surroundings as well as prepare them for a future following a durable solution to their displacement (IDMC, 2010: 6). Education programmes should be developed to enable internally displaced children to re-enter regular education structures, if appropriate (Women's Commission for Refugee Women and Children, 2006: 18).

Through the provision of an education which is available, accessible, acceptable and adaptable, the right to education becomes an 'enabling right', allowing the activation of other political and civil rights. It has thus come to be seen as the fourth pillar of humanitarian assistance and increasing attention is being paid to the role education plays as part of peacebuilding processes or the reconstruction of society following conflict or disaster.

Barriers to Education in Displacement

In some circumstances opportunities for education can increase for children living in displacement. This is most likely to be the case for refugees moving to a country with better educational provision. It may also apply where displacement leads to a loosening of cultural norms which previously restricted access, such as has been the case for Afghan girls in parts of Pakistan. In Chad, data from 185,000 IDPs indicates a decrease in the proportion of out-of-school children (between 61 and 67% in August 2008, compared to 89% a year earlier). In this case the move to UNICEF-managed displacement camps appears to have increased access to formal education (Ferris & Winthrop, 2010: 18). However, these instances are the exception, with available evidence indicating that displacement severely restricts access to education (see Women's Commission for Refugee Women and Children, 2006; Mooney and French, 2005; Dryden-Peterson, 2011; IDMC, 2010). A number of the barriers to accessing education in displacement are similar to the barriers faced in any conflict setting but they impact on those living in displacement through different mechanisms. Barriers include:

- Lack of education infrastructure and resources
  During war schools are often destroyed, either because they are caught in the crossfire or, increasingly, because they are specifically targeted for attack (O'Malley, 2010). Even when they do not suffer damage, schools are usually well-placed to be co-opted for other uses. In Yemen, for example, schools have reportedly been used for military purposes by both Al-Houthi rebels and government forces (IDMC, 2011a: 26). In Pakistan the practice of using schools to house displaced persons deprived both host community and displaced community children of their access to education (IDMC, 2010b: 25). Furthermore, unlike camps which are specifically designed to deal with displaced populations, for those who flee to urban areas the educational provision may simply be unable to deal with the additional children.

Finally, in addition to the impact on physical infrastructure, conflict takes its toll on human resources, with teachers often being forced to flee.

- Safety
The IDMC (2011a) reports that in 2010 children in at least 18 countries faced threats to their physical safety while exercising their right to education. Where there are no schools available in IDP camps or settlements, the journey to and from school can put children at risk of harassment or abduction by armed groups. In Afghanistan threats of sexual violence on the way to school has meant that many internally displaced girls stayed at home (Mooney and French, 2005: 2). Returnees may also be wary of travelling alone as, compared to those who remained in the community throughout conflict, they are less likely to know where landmines have been placed.

- Poverty
The effects of conflict are compounded by increased levels of poverty reported by IDPs. Costs associated with education, including fees, materials and uniforms, can be particularly damaging for IDPs who, having left behind possessions and lost their livelihoods, are unable to meet them. Children may also miss school because they need to work to support their family economically. Internally displaced households in Afghanistan cite child labour as the primary reason for young boys being out of school (Koser and Schmeidl, 2009). In other cases children may need to care for younger siblings so that the mother can work. While the extended family may previously have provided childcare, in displacement the nuclear family often needs to fulfil this role, with the burden often falling on children (Ferris and Winthrop, 2010: 22). Girls are particularly burdened by these responsibilities: much more needs to be done to enable them to stay in school in accordance with Principle 23(3) of the Guiding Principles which calls for special efforts towards the full and equal participation of women and girls in education.

- Discrimination
Whether on the grounds of ethnic differences or the simple fact of being displaced, many IDPs will face discrimination before or during displacement. This can be so pervasive as to limit internally displaced children's access to education. Indigenous and minority IDP students have been turned away even before entering classrooms in Colombia and Mexico (Mooney and French, 2005: 3). Discrimination may even have been on a more institutional level. The IDMC has recently undertaken a number of case studies examining education and displacement. The case of Turkey demonstrates that the government's interpretation of its domestic anti-discrimination law to include only Armenians, Greeks and Jews leaves Kurdish IDPs (who constitute the vast majority) unable to access education which is culturally and linguistically appropriate (IDMC, 2010c). The case study on Georgia (2011c)

demonstrates that discrimination in accessing education may also take the form of segregated schools established for IDPs, impeding their integration into the community. This is especially problematic given the protracted nature of internal displacement in Georgia.

- Loss of documentation
  Certification Counts, an important study led by IIEP-UNESCO (Kirk, 2009). underscores the importance of ensuring the recognition, validation and certification of learning attainments. Displacement frequently results in the loss or confiscation of identity documents. While Guiding Principle 20 affirms the right of IDPs to obtain reissued copies lost in the course of displacement without having to return to their area of origin, obtaining replacement documentation is often very difficult. Without these documents, however, internally displaced children are often unable to enrol in school and internally displaced teachers may be barred from teaching. The loss of educational records may also make it difficult for internally displaced children to enrol in school without having to repeat prior learning and may make it impossible for them to register for state exams (Aguilar and Retamal 1998: 8). As Ferris and Winthrop argue, the longer-term impacts of education in times of crisis, especially in relation to restoring a sense of normality and working towards employment opportunities, are largely compromised when educational attainment is not formally recognized (2010: 24).

- Financing
  Funding remains a major obstacle to ensuring the education of IDPs during crisis. An important initiative has been the formation of the Inter-Agency Network on Education in Emergencies (INEE) led by UNESCO, UNHCR, UNICEF, Norwegian Refugee Council, CARE International and the Save the Children Alliance. This has raised the visibility of education in emergencies, and humanitarian aid for education has nearly doubled since 2006, reaching nearly $450 million as of the CAP revisions in July 2009 (Ferris and Winthrop, 2010: 23). The creation of the education cluster in 2006 has also at times led to the greater inclusion of education as part of humanitarian response: in Sri Lanka the cluster helped ensure that early childhood care was provided in IDP camps and facilitated the distribution of education materials (Papadopoulos 2010). However, education still receives only 2% of humanitarian aid and receives the lowest response to funds requested when compared to food, health, shelter, water and sanitation (UNESCO, 2011: 204). At times competing priorities have caused UNHCR to cut educational programmes mid-year (Ferris and Winthrop, 2010: 23).

National and International Responses: Mapping Actors and Agencies

National Responses

As the Guiding Principles affirm, the responsibility to provide protect and assist IDPs lies with national authorities. The level of commitment to this responsibility varies greatly from one country to the next. Whilst there are over fifty countries with situations of internal displacement, only 17 of these had adopted a national legal framework or policy to protect the rights of IDPs by the end of 2010 (IDMC, 2011a: 32). There is also variation in the degree to which national authorities have begun to implement these policies, with countries such as Nepal having made little progress in putting them into practice (see IDMC, 2011a: 32). However, other countries have not only started to implement their policies, but in a growing number of countries domestic institutions now monitor and guide the government's performance. In Colombia, for example, the Constitutional Court oversees the government's monitoring and reporting of the situation of IDPs compared to the rest of the population. Furthermore, in 2010 the Uganda Human Rights Commission took over from UNHCR the leadership of the group coordinating activities to protect IDPs and promote durable solutions (IDMC, 2011a: 33).

In Africa, there has also been progress in the development of regional mechanisms to provide protection to IDPs. The adoption of the Convention for the Protection and Assistance of IDPs in Africa (the Kampala Convention) by AU member states in October 2009 has been described as 'an historic achievement' (IDMC, 2011a: 33). The Convention is the first regional instrument to impose legal obligations on states to protect and assist IDPs. It applies to contexts of displacement as a result of armed conflict and violence, natural disasters and development projects, and addresses the protection and assistance of IDPs before, during and after displacement. It will come into force once it has been ratified by 15 countries.

With regard to ensuring the right to education in displacement, of the more than 50 countries monitored by the IDMC, only 18 countries have referenced IDP children, either directly or indirectly, in national laws and policies. Of the ten countries with the largest IDP populations, only three have drafted laws or policies about IDP children or youth: Colombia, Iraq and Turkey (Ferris and Winthrop, 2010: 13). Once again, there is variation in the degree to which these policies are implemented (see Ferris and Winthrop, 2010: 13).

International Response

As outlined in the 1998 Guiding Principles, the responsibility to protect IDPs lies primarily with the national authorities. However, in the case where governments are not in a position to ensure this protection, the international community has a duty to ensure that their rights and needs are addressed. Unlike refugees, IDPs do not have a UN agency specifically mandated to assist them. However, there are a number of UN agencies who are tasked with monitoring their needs and providing them with assistance and protection. These include:

- IDMC

  Established by the Norwegian Refugee Council in 1998, the Internal Displacement Monitoring Centre (IDMC) runs an online database providing information and analysis on internal displacement in over fifty countries. The IDMC also plays a strong advocacy role in presenting gaps in national and international responses and carries out training activities to enhance the capacity of actors and agencies to respond to the needs of IDPs.

- UNHCR

  Since 1950 UNHCR has been mandated to lead and coordinate international action to protect the rights and well-being of refugees and stateless people. This includes ensuring that everyone can exercise the right to seek refuge in another state with the opportunity of then returning home voluntarily, integrating into a local community or resettling in a third country (UNHCR, 2011). UNHCR's mandate does not specifically cover IDPs but has assisted them since the 1970s, playing a particularly prominent role in the 1990s, including in the Balkans, the South Caucasus, Colombia and Sri Lanka (Cohen, 2005). However, its response attracted criticism for selectivity (UNHCR, 2007). In September 2005, responding to a call by the General Assembly for more predictable, effective and accountable systems, the UN Inter-Agency Standing Committee (IASC) established the 'cluster approach'. The rationale behind this approach is that there are designated agencies that should be responsible at both the global level as well as the national level during an emergency response to provide enhanced leadership, accountability and predictability of emergency actions in key sectors. UNHCR assumed the lead role for the protection cluster and took responsibility for the coordination and management of IDP camps and emergency shelter. At the end of 2010, 14.7 million IDPs were receiving protection or assistance from UNHCR (UNHCR, 2010:2).

As part of the reforms to humanitarian response, the UN Inter-Agency Standing Committee (IASC) has also established an education cluster which is co-led globally by UNICEF and Save the Children. As of March 2011, forty-two countries have established education clusters, thirty-eight of which are currently active and four are dormant (Global Education Cluster 2011). The cluster has made important progress in putting education in emergencies on the agenda and in improving coordination during humanitarian response. However, Ferris and Winthrop (2010) highlight that there is now some confusion as to which UN agency, UNICEF or UNHCR, is primarily responsible for IDPs. UNHCR seeks to ensure the rights, including education, of 'people of concern to UNHCR'. This includes refugees, asylum-seekers, stateless persons, IDPs and returnees. However, in line with their mandate, UNHCR education staff argue that their priority lies in protecting the right to education for refugees and not for IDPs who should be covered through UNICEF and its responsibilities in the education cluster. This is also compounded by the lack of funding for education activities within UNHCR (Ferris and Winthrop, 2010: 20). In the context of increasing internal displacement, greater clarification is needed around the role education can play in displacement as well as the division of labour between different agencies.

The Chapters

In Chapter 1 Anne Lauten reflects on the United States government's response to Hurricane Katrina and, despite the enormous resources and capacities involved, finds it lacking in a number of regards. The strong militarization of the security response, evident in both the trailer parks and schools, failed to take the context and existing community support systems into account. Despite years of global knowledge-sharing around humanitarian response, the government also failed to apply child protection standards such as 'family unity' and 'continuity'. The ad hoc 'patchwork' of experiments in educational planning failed to take into account the real needs of displaced students. Lauten argues that these failures not only hindered displaced children's full enjoyment of their right to education but also meant the response missed important opportunities for protection that education can provide.

In Chapter 2 Silje Sjøvaag Skeie examines the impact of conflict and displacement on children, and in particular girls' access to education in Puntland and Somaliland. In examining two approaches used by the NRC, an alternative basic education programme for over-age, out-of-school children and a voucher system aimed at supporting formal education, she presents important lessons for improving female enrolment rates in a manner that is sensitive to displaced population and host community relations. The chapter also raises important questions relating to the sustainability of NGO-supported education programmes and the need to ensure buy-in at all levels of society.

Chapter 3 draws on the analysis of the 2011 Global Monitoring Report to examine the distinctive problems faced by IDPs in accessing their right to education in the context of conflict. In this chapter Kevin Watkins outlines what he describes as 'the systematic failure of national governments and the international community to address their needs'. The OECD DAC Principles for good international engagement in fragile states emphasize the need to take context as the starting point, and the chapter alludes to a number of ways in which conflict-induced displacement differs from natural disaster settings. While the primary responsibility to protect and assist IDPs lies with national authorities, governments are more likely to be agents of displacement or implicated in violating the rights of IDPs in the midst of conflict. Secondly, in comparison to natural disasters, conflicts are somewhat more predictable and long-term, with a conflict in a low-income country lasting on average 12 years. Finally, given the links between ethnic fragmentation, inequality and conflict, education has a pivotal role to play in changing attitudes and forging senses of identity that make societies more resilient and less vulnerable to violent conflict. It is in this context that the author argues that current responses, characterized by short-termism, chronic under-financing and divorced from wider peacebuilding processes, are failing internally displaced children worldwide.

Colombia is not only a country with one of the world's largest populations of internally displaced persons worldwide but also the state with the most important contributions by the judiciary to the protection of IDPs. In Chapter 4, Manuel José Cepeda Espinosa examines the process of increasing their legislative protection, as well as specific legal measures undertaken with regard to education, housing, land protection and health. Ultimately, however, the question of how far it is possible to protect IDPs' constitutional rights in the face of continuing conflict remains.

Having suffered a long-standing conflict, a major earthquake and two years of successive flooding, all of which caused repeated and prolonged displacement, Pakistan demonstrates the complexities of a reality characterized by fluidity and change. In Chapter 5 Ferris and Stark examine internally displaced children's access to education in this context. This includes the contrasting experiences of those displaced to camps, who often experienced an increase in access, as well as those who sought refuge in host communities where local systems were unable to manage the influx. The authors argue that a government response which (mistakenly) approached displacement as temporary, combined with the international community's reluctance to prioritise 'education in emergencies', resulted in serious shortcomings in the provision of education for displaced children.

In Chapter 6 Lynn Davies' account of protracted displacement in Sri Lanka highlights that IDP/host-community relations are not static. Her analysis calls into question the category of 'host', arguing that it conceals heterogeneity and fails to locate the individuals within the disparities in power, socio-economic level and gender that characterize the wider population. Education is one part of this political-economic landscape: it is highly valued, and educational deprivation is perceived as a sign and symptom of inequalities of power. A 'return to normality', as promoted in the international response, is therefore not what is needed. Rather, education has a central role to play in peacebuilding strategies and a political-economic approach should be used to identify opportunities in education to break structures of discrimination. Most importantly, the voices of the displaced about education (as well as the voices of their 'hosts') have to be heard clearly in any humanitarian or peacebuilding work.

In post-war Bosnia and Herzegovina the focus has been on promoting the return of IDPs to their area of origin. This is enshrined in the Dayton Peace Agreement which also draws the link between sustainable return and lasting peace. Sixteen years after the war-time ethnic cleansing, however, displaced persons remain reluctant to return to communities in which they would now constitute a demographic minority. In Chapter 7 Perry and Bowder examine the often overlooked role that education plays in this process. They argue that the current system in which Bosniaks, Bosnian Croats and Bosnian Serbs attend separate schools and receive divisive curriculum is not only failing to promote sustainable return and (re)integration of minority returnees, but also preventing the country's long-term democratic consolidation.

In Chapter 8 Alan Smith reflects on a number of developments that have influenced international aid over the past decade and their implications for the provision of education for IDPs. These include arguments for the inclusion of education as part of a humanitarian response, changes to the global security environment, and the implications of UN involvement in peacebuilding. It argues that there is a lack of understanding around the roles education may play in the wake of crisis, as well as the contexts in which people are internally displaced. In the context of increasing internal displacement, this book therefore represents a very important contribution towards greater clarification.

References

Aguilar, P. and G. Retamal (1998), *Rapid Educational Response in Complex Emergencies: A discussion document*. International Bureau of Education.

Castles, S. and N. Van Hear (2005), *Developing DFID's Policy Approach to Refugees and Internally Displaced Persons*. Oxford: Refugees Studies Centre, University of Oxford.

Cohen, R. (2005), 'UNHCR: Expanding its Role with IDPs'. *Forced Migration Review* (23) IDP Supplement

Crisp, J. F. (2002), *No solutions in Sight: the Problem of Protracted Refugee Situations in Africa. San Diego: Centre for Comparative Immigration Studies*. University of California, Working Paper, No. 68.

Dryden-Peterson, S. (2011), 'Conflict, Education and Displacement'. *Conflict and Education 1*(1).

Ferris, E. & Winthrop, R. (2010), *Education and Displacement: Assessing Conditions for Refugees and Internally Displaced Persons affected by Conflict*. Paris: UNESCO.

IASC (2010), *IASC Framework on Durable Solutions for Internally Displaced Persons*. Washington: The Brookings Institution-University of Bern Project on Internal Displacement.

ICRC (2009), *Summary Report: Afghanistan, Colombia, Democratic Republic of the Congo, Georgia, Haiti, Lebanon, Liberia and the Philippines*. Geneva: ICRC.

IDMC (2011a), *Internal Displacement: Global Overview of Trends and Developments in 2010*. Geneva: IDMC.

—(2011b), *Displacement Due to Natural Hazard-Induced Disasters: Global Estimates for 2009 and 2010*. Geneva: IDMC.

—(2011c), *Moving Towards Integration: Overcoming Segregated Education for IDPs. Case Study on Education and Displacement in Georgia*. Geneva: IDMC.

—(2010a), *Learning in Displacement. Briefing Paper on the Right to Education of Internally Displaced People*. Geneva: IDMC.

—(2010b), *Still at Risk. Internally Displaced Children's Rights in North-West Pakistan*. Geneva: IDMC.

—(2010c), *Principle Versus Practice. Case Study on Education and Displacement in Turkey*. Geneva: IDMC.

Kirk, J (ed.) (2009), *Certification Counts: Recognizing the learning attainments of displaced and refugee students*. Paris: International Institute for Educational Planning.

Koser, K. and Schmeidl, S. (2009), 'Displacement, Human Development and Security in Afghanistan', in Amr, H. (ed.) *Displacement in the Muslim World: A Focus on Afghanistan and Iraq*. Washington: Brookings Institution.

Long, K. (2011), *Permanent Crises? Unlocking the Protracted Displacement of Refugees and Internally Displaced Persons*. Oxford: Refugees Studies Centre, University of Oxford.

Montemurro, M. and N. Walicki (2010), 'Invisibility of Urban IDPs in Europe' *Forced Migration Review* (34).

Mooney, E. (2005), 'The Concept of Internal Displacement and the Case for Internally Displaced Persons as a Category of Concern' *Refugee Survey Quarterly* 24(3).

Mooney, E. and C. French (2005), *Access to Education for Internally Displaced Children*. Washington: The Brookings Institution- University of Bern Project on Internal Displacement.

Okello, M. C. and Hovil, L. (2007) 'Confronting the Reality of Gender-based Violence in Northern Uganda' The International Journal of Transitional Justice (1).

O'Malley, B. (2010), *Education Under Attack 2010*. Paris: UNESCO.

Papadopoulos, N. (2010), *Achievements and Challenges of the Education Cluster in the Occupied Palestinian Territory, Somalia and Sri Lanka*. Paris: UNESCO.

UNESCO (2011), *Education for All Global Monitoring Report 2011: The hidden crisis: Armed conflict and education*. Paris: UNESCO.

UNHCR (2007), *The Protection of Internally Displaced Persons and the Role of UNHCR*. Informal Consultative Meeting. [Online] at www.unhcr.org (Accessed Jan 2012).

—(2010), *UNHCR Global Trends 2010*. Geneva: UNHCR.

Women's Commission for Refugee Women and Children (2006), *Right to Education During Displacement. A Resource for Organizations Working with Refugees and Internally Displaced Persons*. New York: Women's Commission for Refugee Women and Children.

1

The Education Sector Response to Hurricane Katrina in the USA

Anne Westbrook Lauten

Chapter Outline

Abstract

Despite enormous resources, forewarning of the event and government systems that remained largely untouched by the disaster, the United States government proved lacking in its response to the humanitarian emergency created by Hurricane Katrina. Displaced Children, in particular, reaped the consequences of the government's missteps, as political decision-making repeatedly ignored international standards and experience in humanitarian response. The following chapter examines the application of child protection principles in the Katrina response, both generally, regarding attention paid to the creation of a protective environment for displaced families, and specifically, highlighting opportunities lost in improving child protection through the education system. Ultimately, opportunities to rebuild a safer, better and more equitable city for New Orleans' children were handicapped by political posturing and misplaced priorities, which ignored both the context in which the disaster occurred and the well-documented lessons of the humanitarian field.

Introduction

In the aftermath of Hurricane Katrina many of the individuals most affected by the disaster took offense to being called refugees[1] by the media. Ironically, the thousands of people who lost their homes, livelihoods and social support networks following Katrina's landfall may have ultimately been more vulnerable due to the fact that they were not legally entitled to refugee status. Being internally displaced persons (IDPs) within the United States meant that the survivors of the hurricane were repeatedly subject to the missteps of the US government at best, and to the arrogance and ignorance of some of its members at worst. Social services in New Orleans were stretched prior to the hurricane. The public education system, in particular, was in crisis (Adamo, 2007) with 73.5% of New Orleans parish schools having been rated 'academically unacceptable' by the state during the 2003–4 school year and 35% of schools not making adequate progress in 2005 according to the No Child Left Behind Act (Hill and Hannaway, 2006: 2). Unfortunately, the 'opportunity' to recreate these services from the ground up after the hurricane was largely squandered as policy makers repeatedly ignored more than 15 years of lessons learned within the humanitarian sector on how to respond to complex emergencies.

While effective solutions to the destruction and displacement created by major catastrophic events depend on a confluence of factors, the immediate response to such events fundamentally lays the groundwork for success or failure of longer term recovery efforts. The government holds the greatest responsibility in defining and executing this first response. Addressing the rights of children following a natural disaster is particularly crucial to ensuring positive long-term outcomes for those children and their families. The following chapter specifically considers attention paid to child protection vis-à-vis children's right to education in the aftermath of Hurricane Katrina. Highlighting international standards in child protection generally, and in education specifically, the chapter considers how lack of planning coupled with policy decisions in the Gulf created and/or reinforced barriers that prevented children from fully realizing this right.

Evolution of Post-Disaster Assistance and Protection of Internally Displaced Persons

Responding to a large-scale natural disaster like Hurricane Katrina has historically proven complicated even for the most well-resourced nations. The assumptions that aid was fundamentally altruistic and positive were destroyed in the responses to complex emergencies of the 1980s and 90s, in which the politics intertwined in the aid efforts often gave rise to devastating impacts on social and institutional structures in affected countries. The Gulf States have been no exception to this trend. As noted by Kates et al.,

> 'For three centuries, New Orleans has had the recurrent opportunities found in other disasters to rebuild the familiar in safer, better and more equitable ways. It essentially rebuilt the familiar, expanded between disasters, and provided marginal increases in safety but laid the groundwork for the next catastrophic failure with major burdens falling on the poor'.
>
> (Kates et al., 2006: 14656)

As the failures in international humanitarian response became increasingly glaring in the late twentieth century, efforts to professionalize the field took hold. Studies had revealed that despite their complexity, disasters shared key characteristics. In 1994, the International Committee for the Red Cross led an effort by non-governmental organizations to identify and define their responsibilities to disaster-affected populations, ultimately articulating a 'Code of Conduct' adopted by the General Assembly of the Red Cross and Red Crescent Societies in 1997. Soon after, the same group of organizations which had helped to create the ICRC Code of Conduct, worked with academics and peers to produce quantifiable minimum 'Sphere Standards' designed to translate the core humanitarian principles of protection and assistance into tangible practice – most notably in the fields of water and sanitation, food security and nutrition, shelter and non-food items and health. Finally, these organizations committed to a 'Humanitarian Charter,' signifying the recognition of the legal rights and responsibilities inherent in humanitarian response. While the Charter is designed to guide the actions of humanitarian agencies, the duties of states and/or warring parties remain primary; humanitarian agency duties are triggered only when state and/or non-state armed actors are either unable or unwilling to meet their humanitarian obligations under law (Sphere 2004: 18). Together, the three documents represent the 'rights-based' approach to humanitarianism. They focus on the rights of the affected population and the responsibilities of governments and, secondarily, humanitarian agencies to protect lives while promoting wellbeing.

While education has developed more recently as a priority in humanitarian response, child protection has long been viewed as an essential element of the initial response to a crisis. Two key principles have specifically emerged in child protection practice, complementing the core humanitarian commitment to providing protection and assistance to disaster-affected populations: (1) the principle of family unity and (2) the 'continuity principle' (Omer and Alon, 1994). The first principle requires actors involved in humanitarian response to consider children who have been separated from their families as 'among the most vulnerable' (International Committee of the Red Cross, 2004: 2), and to ensure that any humanitarian action makes every effort to respect the family as an inseparable unit. The 'continuity principle' goes one step further, focusing on the importance of maintaining the child's existing individual, familial, organization and communal strengths and resources in order to counteract the disruptive effects of disaster (Klingman, 2002).

Although the right to education is codified in the Universal Declaration of Human Rights (1948), the Convention on the Rights of the Child (1989), the Guiding Principles on Internal Displacement, the American Declaration on the Rights and Duties of Man (1998), as well as a number of other key international and regional conventions and agreements, this right has often been classified as 'secondary' to life-saving priorities highlighted in the Sphere Standards. However, through the 1990s, the protective quality of education began to receive greater attention in child protection circles. The child protection framework aspires to reduce risks to a child's social and psychological development, and to enhance the enabling external and environmental factors, which can foster and support a child's wellbeing in the face of adversity (Dawes and Donald, 1994: 19). In recent years, the child protection community has increasingly looked to education institutions to support child resiliency to catastrophic events. In 2004, the Inter-Agency Network for Education in Emergencies published a companion to the Sphere Standards providing minimum standards for education in emergencies. The INEE Minimum Standards focus specifically on ensuring community partici-pation, providing an education system that is grounded in rigorous analysis of needs and strategy for action, ensuring that access to schooling is safe and non-discriminatory, and that educators are qualified, and supported to provide learner-centered appropriate and relevant instruction. Finally, the INEE Minimum Standards address policies around education, requiring flexibility in emergencies to promote inclusion and quality education, but ensuring information sharing with relevant stakeholders, addressing the specific needs of the displaced population and providing quality education in line with national and international standards. Education, in particular, was seen to offer children a sense of self-worth that comes with being identified as a student, to support the growth and development of social networks, and to provide a structure and order to an otherwise often chaotic environment (Nicolai and Tripplehorn, 2003: 9). Recognizing these important benefits, guidance on the protection of IDPs has increasingly included specific instruction on ensuring the right to education in emergencies.

Child Protection and Education in the Wake of Hurricane Katrina

The response to Hurricane Katrina effectively highlights the two key intersections of child protection and education in emergencies. On the one hand, strong education systems may have the capacity to respond to child protection concerns in the aftermath of a disaster. On the other hand, a lack of attention to the basic tenets of child protection throughout the response can seriously penalize efforts to ensure safe and equitable access to education. The response to Hurricane Katrina revealed extreme weakness on both fronts. The education system in the Gulf region was far from strong at the time the hurricane hit, after being crippled by years of mismanagement and poor performance. As of August 2005, the school district of New Orleans Parish alone was facing a more than $25 million deficit (Hill and Hannaway, 2006). The hurricane then added to the burden, rendering unusable 16 of the previous 126 public schools in New Orleans parish and more than 600 schools in the region (Harvard Educational Review, 2005). A patchwork of policies designed to 'fix' the education system generally left more than 370,000 displaced students with relatively few options, most of which did little to prioritize quality education or provide greater protection to students.

The response to Hurricane Katrina also failed to capitalize on more general global learning in child protection, resulting in children being repeatedly exposed to risks to their wellbeing throughout the recovery effort. Specifically, efforts by the government to secure the affected area took on an 'us-against-them' persona, creating a militarized environment in which many residents felt more threatened than secure. The temporary housing of displaced residents was poorly planned and poorly executed, forcing families to move multiple times and causing significant disruption to any efforts they made to resume their 'normal' lives. Finally, despite initial proclamations that the reconstruction of the gulf region presented great opportunities to create 'better' communities, those opportunities were rapidly subsumed by competing pressures to rebuild quickly regardless of quality, poor communication and collaboration between different levels of the government and a complete lack of consistent and reliable communication with the affected population. As poor decisions in the field of child protection immediately following the hurricane were compounded by 'experiments' to fix the education system in New Orleans, the few positive opportunities that Hurricane Katrina may have created were largely squandered.

Creating a Protective Environment for IDPs in the Aftermath of Katrina

While 'protection' describes actions that prevent and respond to a wide range of rights concerns, it is fundamentally grounded in creating an environment in which individuals are safe. In a typical response to disaster a number of security measures are taken to ensure such a protective environment: police or security monitors[2] are positioned in areas that are known to pose hazards to the civilian population; displacement and refugee camps are disarmed; and safe living environments for children are promoted by ensuring that living facilities and social organization arrangements consider needs for privacy, adequate space, sufficient lighting at night, etc. (UN High Commissioner for Refugees, 1994: 53–4). Reestablishing the rule of law is essential to creating the space for displaced populations to regain a sense of normality in their lives. Furthermore, the order that is inherent in widespread respect for the rule of law typically opens the space for government agencies to provide effectively essential social services to the population in support of the more general recovery of the affected region.

The areas hardest hit by Hurricane Katrina were known for significant violence long before Katrina struck. In 2003, murder, rape, robbery, aggravated assault, burglary, larceny and motor vehicle theft all occurred at levels greater than the US national average (Crime Rating, 2003). In a study carried out by Save the Children with 700 displaced students in two Baton Rouge schools immediately following Katrina, roughly 60% had witnessed a shooting or murder prior to the hurricane. Nearly half the children interviewed had seen a drug sale, one third had witnessed a shooting, and 42% had seen physical violence between a man and a woman[3]. Furthermore, nearly one-fifth of the children had witnessed all three forms of violence, and one third had been exposed to two of the three (Lauten and Lietz, 2008: 171). Such statistics are useful in highlighting the vulnerability of the hurricane-affected population, in that many affected individuals – including children – had been repeatedly exposed to traumatic events. Ultimately, such exposure makes coping with the effects of catastrophic events like Katrina significantly more difficult.

The extreme militarization in the security response to Katrina, with political leaders equating the 'security threat' in New Orleans with the War on Terror,[4] only served to exacerbate this difficulty further. As noted by Binu et al., the common assumption that natural disasters trigger mass disruption, disorder and social breakdown is not only false but that 'it is well documented that natural and man-made disasters are followed by increases in altruistic behavior and social solidarity' (Binu et al., 2008: 558). Unfortunately, although the government did actively address security post-Katrina, it did so without significant understanding of or regard for the population it was meant to be protecting. The government's approach to security focused on numbers. As of the beginning of September there were a total of 14,232 active duty military personnel and 22,000 members of the National Guard in the Gulf Coast region – primarily in New Orleans (White House, 2006: 43). At that time, more than half the residents of the affected region had left the area, meaning that with the influx of military personnel in September 2005, there was approximately one member of the military for every five civilian residents.[5] The commitment to a security presence continued beyond the initial response to the hurricane, when large numbers of highly paid, primarily out-of-state security guards were brought into the area by the Federal Emergency Management Agency (FEMA) as well as agencies responsible for social services.

Yet, even with such a security presence, 49% of residents in FEMA-supported trailer parks reported that they did not feel safe walking in their community at night and 45% did not feel comfortable letting their children play in the trailer parks during the day. Additionally, 25% believed that their children had been newly exposed to drugs or alcohol during displacement (International Medical Corps, 2006: 5). Adamo notes that the new public school system paid for one security guard per 37 students, in stark contrast with the 1:333 pre-Katrina ratio, but still failed to provide real security for these schools, resulting in vandalism, theft and danger to the surrounding community (Adamo, 2007).

What the US Government did not capitalize on in its security response to Hurricane Katrina were the coping strategies of a population already familiar with serious security threats. The population most affected by the Hurricane was extremely rooted in New Orleans, meaning that individuals were able to rely on long-standing personal relationships and knowledge of their community to navigate security threats to themselves and their families. When individuals develop attachments to other people (such as friends, teachers or religious leaders), pets, objects and places, proximity to these objects of attachment can influence the perception of danger and can reduce fear. As such, separation from loved ones and familiar surroundings can be a greater stressor than the physical danger itself (Binu et al., 2008: 563). The organization of displaced communities, including ensuring their access to stabilizing social services, is therefore a key element in creating a protective environment for the displaced.

The tragedy of the Katrina response was that pre-existing social networks could have been preserved and used. While displacement of the Gulf residents did not need to equate the mass dispersal of those residents, opportunities to maintain communities were largely ignored. Unfortunately, when the federal and state governments were faced with the opportunity to design effectively communities in the Gulf, responding agencies proved sorely lacking in their attention to protective social networks that had been previously established by displaced residents. First, in the immediate aftermath of the hurricane, criteria for housing support from the federal government left the most vulnerable populations wanting. Those families that resided in rental accommodations – the equivalent of more than half the affected population – were *not* eligible for permanent housing assistance. Over the longer term, FEMA dedicated more than $3 billion to establishing massive trailer park communities, but was ultimately incapable of responding to the massive needs of the displaced. In addition to delays in getting trailer parks set up, resistance by host communities to the influx of displaced residents led FEMA to locate many of the trailer parks in outlying areas far from basic social services and without access to public transportation. At the other extreme, FEMA trailers were dispersed among pre-existing trailer parks, where parents reported that a cold reception by pre-hurricane residents kept them unwilling to allow their children to play outside and children feeling unwanted in local schools (Lauten and Lietz 2008: 183).

The organization of communities post-disaster plays an essential role in the degree to which stability can be re-established in a child's life. Social connectedness at the family, community and societal level is a key element in children's resilience to traumatic events (Lerner and Castellino, 2002). These truths have pushed governments and aid organizations to pay particular attention to the design of displaced communities following natural disasters worldwide. Shelters are typically clustered around communal spaces, including community centers, schools and health posts. Over the past two decades, institutional learning has shown the value of specifically ensuring safe spaces for children which allow them to meet, play and interact with peers. Surprisingly, efforts to promote community support systems were almost entirely lacking in the response to Hurricane Katrina.

Katrina was marked by a notable lack of attention to the potential negative effects of displacement, and the negative effects of the break in ties to their community of origin in particular. Clear race and class differences in the ability of residents to leave the city and to benefit from post-disaster assistance left entire communities ignored and abandoned by their government. Initial separations of children from their families – typical in any large scale natural disaster – could not be effectively addressed due to an over-reliance on contextually inappropriate systems for family tracing.[6] Generally poor planning and, considering the predictability of the disaster, an incredible lack of preparedness at all levels of government meant that even 'systems' that were in place were inadequate for responding to the scale of destruction and displacement. Individuals who sought refuge in the larger, but overcrowded and less sanitary FEMA-approved shelters generally received more immediate assistance, while individuals who sought refuge with friends and families and in smaller or makeshift shelters (such as in churches or schools) were often better protected as they typically had a greater level of privacy and safety. Over the medium term a lack of stable housing options for evacuees was just one indication of the inadequate attention to safe living environments for the displaced. In a survey of 253 displaced children carried out by Save the Children, over 20% reported moving four or more times in the three months following the hurricane, while only 15% of respondents reported only one move. Moreover, 37% of the children interviewed reported attending more than one school between August and November (Lauten and Lietz, 2008: 169). Those families that did manage to move into the FEMA trailer parks were forced to forgo prior attachments to their communities as there were no efforts made to keep communities together in the design of the trailer parks, and displaced residents had no choice as to where they were moved. Forced displacement can have a variety of negative effects on the well being of individuals who are subjected to it. Repeated displacement and the unavailability of longer-term solutions – as was the case for many Gulf residents post Katrina – compound those effects, progressively breaking down individuals' capability of coping effectively with the stress brought on by the event.

Education Post-Katrina: A Series of Failures

The response to Hurricane Katrina was somewhat unique among complex emergencies in that state and national capacity to respond to the disaster was largely untouched by the hurricane. While some local offices of government agencies were flooded, they were generally able to be relocated rather than shut down. Unfortunately, any benefit that may have been drawn from the physical presence of government was overshadowed by the poor functioning of the government agencies. The education sector was a particular casualty of the post-Katrina chaos in the US government. The well-intended excitement at the possibility of 'experimenting' with the education sector post-Katrina proved to be the Achilles heel of the various government agencies involved. When coupled with frequent decision-making grounded in politics over sound reasoning and the lack of communication and coordination among agencies, good intentions were simply not enough to allow the education system to provide positive support to students affected by the hurricane. Not only did policy-makers overshoot in their ambition to revamp the New Orleans public school system, they all but forgot to consider the real needs of the city's students.

Supporting education for students displaced by Hurricane Katrina was immediately handicapped by the organization of displacement sites. The overreliance on short-term housing in the months that followed Katrina as a result of the lack of safe and available longer-term options meant that students were often required to change schools as frequently as their families moved. Generally, having to start over at each new school would negate any normalizing effect of school attendance for students, instead reinforcing children's sense of displacement. Displaced students who were lodged with their families in hotels by the government faced an even larger obstacle, as they were frequently blocked from school registration due to the fact that their lodging was 'non-permanent'. Those families that were placed in trailers also faced significant obstacles to enrolling their children in school. A number of the trailer parks were located outside official school zones, creating confusion about where park residents should be registered, as well as logistical difficulties when trailer parks were not located on pre-determined school bus routes. In total, approximately 50,000 students faced obstacles great enough to keep them out of school during the 2005–6 school year, and an estimated 15,000 did not attend during the 2006–7 school year (Save the Children, 2010a).

As is typical in disaster settings, the education system in the Gulf region also suffered a significant blow from Katrina. Many school facilities were destroyed by the hurricane, and those that were not were ordered to be emptied in line with a FEMA policy to protect returning students from the threat of illness due to mould. The irony in the implementation of this policy was that much of the destroyed equipment was not only new, but frequently not damaged, while some of the most badly flooded schools remained untouched safety hazards well into the following year (Adamo, 2007). The US Department of Education released almost $2 billion to support education in the Gulf and education support for displaced students elsewhere in the United States (Department of Homeland Security, 2008). While a large part of this funding was directed at the reconstruction of school infrastructure, a significant portion of the money also went to expensive out-of-state consultants and contractors to support the post-Katrina shift to a predominantly charter school system in New Orleans. This immediate shift to an 'all schools as charter schools' system proved impossible, given the education needs of the affected area. As such, over 100 low-performing schools were regrouped in a state-run 'Recovery District'. Selective admissions criteria for the chartered schools that did open, as well as ongoing performance benchmarks for students attending charter schools, meant that students who were already marginalized and/or underperforming academically – including displaced students – were those least likely to receive the support they needed from the education system, as they were once again relegated to the periphery and 'dumped' in the Recovery School District.

Finally, Katrina was used as an opportunity to try to improve the quality of education in New Orleans. In line with this goal, all former public school teachers were initially laid off following the hurricane. Those who had not been rehired by early 2006 were permitted to reapply as employees at will.

Through a series of tests and interviews – carried out by a private organization, and widely criticized – the pool 500 individuals who applied was reduced to 100 'qualified' teachers (Polier, 2006: 20). Ultimately schools that did reopen – particularly those under the Recovery School District – were overcrowded but staffed with a third too few teachers to maintain a minimally acceptable teacher student ratio (Adamo, 2007). Furthermore, those teachers that were working received only minimal support. While the former teachers union had long been criticized as being corrupt, the new system created enormous flexibility in the management of schools, but left teachers with very little room to influence that management.

The government did show significant flexibility in loosening requirements for schools to adhere to education standards in the Gulf region, ostensibly recognizing the challenges both educators and students faced in the aftermath of Katrina. The federal government permitted the reallocation of funding to target the greatest needs within Louisiana and Mississippi, and gave state governments the flexibility to allocate funding to school districts between areas with large displaced populations and those most damaged by the hurricane as it felt was necessary (Harvard Educational Review, 2005). Unfortunately, the flexibility in the application of education standards ultimately proved to be less about improving access to quality education for students and more about just getting through. At one point the Recovery School District even introduced, and ultimately repealed after heavy criticism, a policy that made it nearly impossible for a student to receive a failing grade. For all the hype about improving quality, a disparate conglomeration of school systems and management structures, hiring and firing practices, and overreliance on outsider 'innovation' and counsel ultimately wasted the 'opportunity' to improve upon the school system that Katrina wiped out.

Education and Child Development Outcomes

Education is protective insofar as it provides a safe environment for students, it offers structure and routine that is essentially normalizing and offers a sense of 'future.' It can bolster a student's confidence and self-worth, and it provides students with the knowledge and skills to be able to analyze information, express opinions and take action. The Katrina response within the education sector proved lacking on each of these fronts. While there was a significant security presence both in trailer parks and in schools, this presence ultimately created more of a police state, in which residents reported feeling threatened and bullied more than safe and protected. Poor student-teacher ratios meant that identifying students with greater needs for support was necessarily more difficult. The structure and routine that education often provides to IDPs was largely absent due to policies that forced families to move repeatedly, as well as those which required parents and students to navigate a complicated and unfamiliar school system. Finally, despite large-scale funding earmarked for schools in the hurricane affected area, complicated and numerous bureaucratic blockages resulted in schools that were inadequately resourced for offering high quality education.

Conclusion

Internationally, standards in education and child protection in emergencies have developed over the past two decades due, in part, to the recognition that humanitarian emergencies are often defined by both the pressure for a quick response and the collapse of national government capacities. While there are inherent opportunities in rebuilding post-disaster, history has repeatedly shown that 'experimenting' with those opportunities – as was done post-Katrina – should be limited. Furthermore, any policy, whether experimental or not, needs to reflect an understanding of context and the population it is designed to support. By ignoring both key contextual specificities about the affected area and international standards in both child protection and education, government agencies responding to Katrina denied the displaced children of the Gulf States the benefit of global learning in its immediate response to the hurricane. Instead these children were victim to one poorly designed strategy after another. In the end, it is difficult to find a good excuse for the failures of the Katrina response. For all its imperfections, the United States government is considerably more functional than many national governments around the world that are faced with natural disasters. Furthermore the response to Katrina was well funded, and the affected areas were accessible almost immediately following the hurricane. Finally, whether in information sharing, in the targeting of vulnerable populations, or in the long term recovery from disasters, decades of experience have informed international protocols for all aspects of disaster response. Combined, it is these factors that made the mammoth mistakes in the government decision-making post-Katrina so unfathomable. It is also these factors which make it so essential for the US government and the humanitarian community to learn from the mistakes that were made.

> ## Questions for Further Discussion
>
> Six years after Hurricane Katrina what are the residual effects of the decisions taken early on in the recovery process?
>
> In what ways do political processes impact upon decisions being made in the immediate aftermath of disaster?
>
> What are the long-term impacts of children's exposure to risk factors – such as displacement, availability of and access to education, etc. – in the immediate aftermath of natural disaster?

Notes

1 As defined in both international and US immigration law, a refugee is a person who owing to well-founded fear of being persecuted for reasons of race, religion, nationality, membership of a particular social group or political opinion, is outside the country of his nationality and is unable, or, owing to such fear, is unwilling to avail himself of the protection of that country; or who, not having a nationality and being outside the country of his former habitual residence as a result of such events, is unable or, owing to such fear, is unwilling to return to it. Conversely, internally displaced persons (IDPs) are persons or groups of persons who have been forced or obliged to flee or leave their homes or places of habitual residence, in particular as a result of or in order to avoid the effects of armed conflict, situations of generalized violence, violations of human rights or natural or human-made disasters, and who have not crossed an internationally recognized state border. Clearly, it is the latter designation and not the more emotionally laden term, refugee, which applies to Katrina survivors.

2 In many cases, increasing a police force is neither possible nor recommended in international contexts. However, in cases where national law enforcement is not a reliable mechanism for ensuring the security of civilians, agencies such as UNHCR, and the UN Department of Safety and Security have a mandate to monitor the security situation, and respond to threats. In these cases, the highest priority is given to investigating and responding to violations of children's rights.

3 The specific question stated, 'Have you seen a man hit a woman?'

4 See United States President. (2005). 'President Discusses Hurricane Relief in Address to the Nation.' New Orleans. [Online]. Available: www.whitehouse. gov/news/releases/2005/09/20050915-8.html

5 Based on initial census information from four months following the Hurricane, New Orleans had 158,353 residents. See Frey, W. H. and A. Singer. (2006). Katrina and Rita Impacts on Gulf Coast Populations: First Census Findings. Brookings Institution. [Online] Available www. brookings.edu/metro/pubs/20060607_hurricanes.pdf.   Assuming   this number includes a small percentage of individuals who returned to the area between September and December 2005, the ratio of military personnel to civilians is approximately 1:5.

6 Despite technological systems that would have allowed children to be effectively registered and reunited with families, authorities initially resorted to traditional message boards, typically used only in extremely remote contexts. Even when internet message boards were introduced, minimal effort was made to ensure that the displaced had sufficient access to these message boards. Finally, even where internet message boards were available, their effectiveness was limited due to the lack of assistance available to those individuals – notably children – who were unable to master the technology on their own.

References

Adamo, Ralph (2006), 'Squeezing Public Education: History and Ideology Gang Up in New Orleans' in *Dissent Magazine*, Summer [Online] Available www.dissentmagazine.org/article/?article=862 (Accessed 4 February 2012).

Binu, Jacob, Anthony R. Mawson, Marinelle Payton and John C. Guignard (2008), 'Disaster Mythology and Fact: Hurricane Katrina and Social Attachment' in *Public Health Reports.* 125 (5), 555–66.

Boothby, N., J. Crawford, and J. Halperin (2006), 'Mozambique Child Soldier Life Outcome Study: Lessons Learned in Rehabilitation and Reintegration Efforts' *Global Public Health*, 1(1), 87–107.

Convention on the Rights of the Child, adopted 20 Nov. 1989, entered into force 2 Sept. 1990, G.A. Res. 44/25, 44 UN GAOR, Supp. (No. 49), UN Doc. A/44/49, at 166 (1989), reprinted in 28 ILM 1448 (1989). 191 states parties.

Dawes, Andrew, and David Donald (1994), *Childhood and Adversity: Psychological Perspectives from South African Research.* South Africa: David Philip Publishers.

Department of Homeland Security (2008), *The First Year after Katrina: What the Federal Government Did.* [Online] Available www.dhs.gov/xfoia/archives/gc_1157649340100.shtm (Accessed 2 December 2011).

Frey, W. H. and A. Singer. (2006), 'Katrina and Rita Impacts on Gulf Coast Populations: First Census Findings.' Brookings Institution Metropolitan Policy Program. [Online] Available www.brookings. edu/metro/pubs/20060607_hurricanes.pdf (Accessed 2 February 2012).

Harvard Educational Review (2005), 'Katrina and Rita: What Can the United States Learn from International Experiences with Education and Displacement.' Winter. [Online] Available hepg.org/her/issue/2 (Accessed 12 December 2011).

Hill, Paul and J. Hannaway (2006), 'The Future of Public Education in New Orleans.' in Turner, Margret Austin and Zedlewski (eds) *After Katrina: Rebuilding Opportunity and Equity into the New New Orleans.* The Urban Institute [Online] Available www.urban.org/UploadedPDF/311406_after_katrina.pdf (Accessed 12 December 2011).

Inter-Agency Network for Education in Emergencies. (2004), *Minimum standards on education in emergencies, chronic crisis and early reconstruction.* New York. [Online] Available www.ineesite. org/uploads/documents/store/Minimum_Standards_2010_eng.pdf (Accessed 11 November 2011).

Inter-Agency Standing Committee. (1999), *Protection of Internally Displaced Persons: Inter-Agency Standing Committee Policy Paper.* New York.

—(2006), *Protecting Persons Affected by Natural Disasters: IASC Operational Guidelines on Human Rights and Natural Disaster.* Washington: Brookings-Bern Project on Internal Displacement.

International Committee of the Red Cross. (2004), *Interagency Guiding Principles on Unaccompanied and Separated Children.* Geneva. Available: www.unhcr.org/cgi-bin/texis/vtx/refworld/rwmain/opendocpdf.pdf?docid=4113abc14 (Accessed 3 January 2012).

International Covenant on Economic, Social and Cultural Rights, adopted 16 Dec. 1966, entered into force 3 Jan. 1976, G. A. Res. 2200A (XXI), UN Doc. A/6316 (1966), 993 UNTS 3, reprinted in 6 ILM 360 (1967). 142 states parties.

International Federation of Red Cross and Red Crescent Societies. (No date), *Principles of Conduct for the International Red Cross and Red Crescent Movement and NGOs in Disaster Response Programmes*, [Online]. Available: www.ifrc.org/publicat/conduct/index.asp?navid=09_08 (Accessed 12 December 2011).

International Medical Corps. (2006), *Displaced in America: Health Status Among Internally Displaced Persons in Louisiana and Mississippi Travel Trailer Parks.* Washington. Available: www. imcworldwide.org/images/File/PDF/Displaced_in_America.pdf (Accessed 11 November 2011).

Kates, R. W., C. E. Colton, S. Laska, and S. P. Leatherman. (2006), 'Reconstruction of New Orleans after Hurricane Katrina: A Research Perspective.' *Proceedings of the National Academy of Sciences of the United States of America,* 103 (40), 14653–14660.

Klingman, A. (2002), 'Children under stress of war' in La Greca, A. M., W. S. Silverman, E. M. Vernberg, and M. C. Roberts (eds), *Helping children cope with disasters and terrorism* (p. 359–80). Washington, DC: American Psychological Association.

Lauten, Anne Westbrook and Kimberly Lietz. (2008), 'A Look at the Standards Gap: Comparing Child Protection.' Responses in the Aftermath of Hurricane Katrina and the Indian OceanTsunami' in *Children Youth and Environments.* Spring 2008: 18(2): 158–201.

Lerner, R. M. and D. R. Castellino. (2002), 'Contemporary developmental theory and adolescence: Developmental Systems and Applied Developmental Science; in *Journal of Adolescent Health 31(6) (supplement):* 122–35.

Nicolai, Susan and Carl Tripplehorn. (2003), 'The Role of Education in Protecting Children in Conflict' *Humanitarian Practice Network,* London: Overseas Development Institute. [Online] Available www.odihpn.org/documents/networkpaper042.pdf (Accessed 11 November 2011).

Omer, H. and N. Alon. (1994), 'The Continuity Principle: A Unified Approach to Disaster and Trauma' in *American Journal of Community Psychology* 22(2): 273–86.

Polier, Nicole. (2006), 'After Katrina: Tales from a Chartered School Classroom' in *The Radical Teacher* 76, 20–3.

Save the Children. (2010a), *Five Years After Katrina, US Remains Unprepared to Protect Children During Disasters* [Online] Available www.savethechildren.org/site/apps/nlnet/content2.aspx?c=8r KLIXMGIpI4E&b=6230287&ct=8643773 (Accessed 12 November 2011).

—(2010b), *A National Report Card on Protecting Children During Disasters* [Online] Available www.savethechildren.org/atf/cf/%7B9def2ebe-10ae-432c-9bd0-df91d2eba74a%7D/ 2010-Disaster-Report.pdf (Accessed 10 November 2011).

The White House (2006), *The Federal Response to Hurricane Katrina: Lessons Learned* [Online]. Available: www.whitehouse.gov/reports/katrina-lessons-learned/ (Accessed 11 November 2011).

United Nations High Commissioner for Refugees (1994), *Refugee Children: Guidelines on Protection and Care.* Geneva: United Nations High Commissioner for Refugees.

United States President (2005), *President Discusses Hurricane Relief in Address to the Nation.* New Orleans. [Online]. Available: www.whitehouse.gov/news/releases/2005/09/20050915-8.html (Accessed January 8, 2006).

Wisner, B. and P. Walker (2005), 'Katrina and Goliath: why the greatest military and economic power in the world didn't protect New Orleans' in *Humanitarian Practice Network.* London: Overseas Development Institute 46–7.

Zimmerman, Marc A. and Revathy Arunkumar. (1994), 'Resiliency Research: Implications for Schools and Policy' in *Social Policy Report,* Society for Research in Child Development, 8(4), 1–17.

Alternative Approaches to Education for Displaced Children in Puntland and Somaliland

2

Silje Sjøvaag Skeie

Chapter Outline

Abstract

After more than twenty years of conflict, Somalia's education indicators are among the worst in the world, and more than three-quarters of Somalia's children and youth are denied their right to education. Internally displaced children, and particularly girls, are among the most marginalized. Since the formal school system is largely unable to adapt to the needs of internally displaced children, alternative education approaches are needed to encourage their participation. This chapter elaborates on the barriers to education for IDPs and particularly for girls. It also discusses two approaches used by the Norwegian Refugee Council[1] to promote effective learning in Puntland and Somaliland; an alternative basic education (ABE) program for over-age, out-of-school children and a voucher system aiming at supporting education through public schools.

Two Decades of Instability: Displacement in Somalia

Two decades after the fall of the previous President of Somalia, Siyad Barre, Somalia is still considered one of the world's most severe humanitarian crises. With more than a quarter of Somalia's population displaced, Somalia is widely acknowledged to have one of the worst displacement situations in the world today (UNHCR, 2011a).

According to the Internal Displacement Monitoring Centre (IDMC), internally displaced persons (IDPs) represent about 16% of the total Somali population. The number of IDPs stood at 1.46 million people in April 2011. The causes of displacement in Somalia are multiple, ranging from flight from armed conflict, loss of livelihood to drought. While the majority of Somalia's displaced are found within Somali territory, a large proportion of Somalia's displaced population live as refugees in neighboring countries (IDMC/RSC, 2011).

Somalia still has IDPs from the first big wave of displacement in 1988 – 1991, when up to two million people were internally displaced and approximately 1.5 million people fled the country (DRC, 2007; Cabdi, 2005). From the mid-1990s to mid-2000, a period of relative stability followed, but with protracted displacement and limited return. At the end of 2000, intensified conflict, drought and famine in the Horn of Africa again led to considerable numbers of IDPs and refugees fleeing south-central Somalia for other parts of the Somali territory and neighboring Kenya and Ethiopia (IDMC/RSC, 2011).

After the collapse of the Republic of Somalia in 1991, the country has moved towards forming autonomous regions. The most pronounced are the self-declared autonomous Republic of Somaliland in the North West, the self-governing Puntland State of Somalia in the North East, and south-central Somalia, governed by the Transitional Federal Government supported by African Union forces, AMISOM. While Puntland does not seek international recognition as a sovereign state, Somaliland aims for independence, but has yet to obtain international recognition (Bradbury, 2008; Lewis, 2009; IDMC/ RSC, 2011). The majority of IDPs are in south-central Somalia[2], but significant numbers are found in the relatively stable areas of Puntland (139,000) and Somaliland (67, 000) (UNHCR Somalia, April 2011).

Who is an IDP in Somalia?

Defining who is an internally displaced person in the context of Somalia is challenging. First, nearly all Somalis have been displaced at some point, and there seems to be consensus among Somalis that most of them do not live in their 'ideal home' (DRC, 2007:5). This brings up the question of when displacement ends. Further, more than half the Somali population are nomadic pastoralists or have nomadic affiliation. Even though many today live at least part of the time in urban centers, the nomadic lifestyle of herding camels, sheep and goats results in a high level of movement (Bradbury 2008, Lewis, 2009). As nomadic migration is sometimes linked to drought and instability, nomads are subject to forceful displacement, raising the question of whether they are in fact internally displaced.

The tendency of IDPs to settle in urban areas makes it difficult to differentiate them from the host community. The majority of the IDPs are integrated with poor urban populations in informal settlements in and around urban centers, often in abandoned buildings or squatting on land owned by locals. Many have integrated locally and therefore consider themselves as local citizens which makes the label 'IDP' unsuitable. Host community households in the vicinity of IDP settlements may also consider the distinction unsuitable and many report being IDPs as they host displaced clan members or as a strategy to access humanitarian assistance (DRC, 2007; IDMC/RSC, 2011; NRC, 2010).

The disintegration of Somalia into three main areas has complicated the picture further. An internally displaced person is a person subject to involuntary movement within national borders and the primary responsibility for ensuring that the needs of IDPs are met lies with the national authorities (UNOCHA, 2004; Brookings, 2010). Due to the lack of international recognition of Somaliland as an independent state, people displaced to Somaliland from other parts of Somalia are considered to be IDPs by the international community. The Authorities of Somaliland, however, regard them as refugees or aliens having crossed an international border. This represents a barrier to durable solutions, for instance making local integration difficult by denying the displaced legal purchase of land. IDPs to Puntland are not faced with the same problem. Since Puntland considers itself a regional state of Somalia displaced persons from south and central are considered IDPs with equal rights as locals (IDMC/RSC, 2011). The relative stability in Somaliland and Puntland provides internally displaced persons with some level of protection and greater access to humanitarian assistance than in the war-ravaged south.

As demonstrated, due to the complexity of the context there are challenges to defining people as internally displaced in Somalia. There are also concerns that defining people as long-term IDPs for the sake of providing humanitarian assistance may in fact encourage self-identification as IDPs and work against integration and finding a durable solution. Yet it can be argued that displaced persons, especially those newly displaced, have particular needs and vulnerabilities which justify the use of the term as well as targeted assistance to this group (DRC, 2007; NRC, 2008; NRC, 2010; IDMC/RSC, 2011).

The Education Sector in Somalia

Education is a fundamental right, for all children in all circumstances. Displacement often leads to violation of this right as education is denied or disrupted. With displacement lasting on average 20 years, internally displaced children and youth risk growing up without any education opportunities (IDMC, 2010). The Global Monitoring Report on Education for All 2011 'The hidden crisis; armed conflict and education' states that internally displaced children and youth are among the most vulnerable in terms of having their education rights denied (UNESCO, 2011).

Somalia is no exception. More than two decades of instability have had a devastating impact on the already weak education system in the Horn of Africa. Across the Somali territory, almost every school was destroyed or damaged, teachers and learners were displaced and education materials were burned or looted. Continued instability, lack of government capacity and limited budgets have hampered restoration of the education system. The authorities of Puntland and Somaliland have made significant progress in advancing the education sector since the end of the war in 1991, but challenges of lack of access and poor education quality remain. Accurate statistics do not exist but the most recent numbers indicate Gross Enrollment Rate (GER) in Somaliland at 39% and in Puntland at 40% (Somaliland Ministry of Education, 2007a, Puntland MOE), which is among the lowest in the world.

Commitment to formal education has traditionally been low in Somali society. Prior to colonial rule Somali children were educated informally in their homes, and the first school in Somaliland opened as late as 1943, during British colonial rule (Cabdi, 2005). Since Somalis are predominantly Muslims, many parents prefer to send their children to Quranic schools (*dugsi*), where recitation of the Holy Quran is taught, rather than to formal schools. Dugsi education does not fall under the responsibility of the Ministry of Education.

More and more children attend both *dugsi* and public schools, and there is an increasing demand for 'integrated education', combining formal and religious education (NRC, 2011). There are also a growing number of private schools, especially in urban areas, but they are only accessible to well-off families.

The lack of accurate statistics combined with the challenge of distinguishing IDPs from the host population, makes it difficult to state to what extent IDPs are marginalized in education. A comprehensive IDP profiling exercise conducted by the Danish Refugee Council (DRC) in 2007 indicated that internally displaced children participate slightly less in education compared to the overall population. Twenty-four per cent of IDP children in Bossaso, Puntland attended school compared to 40% of the host population (DRC/ UNHCR, 2007b). In Burao, Somaliland, the trend was less evident, with 37.5% of IDP children attending school compared to 39% (DRC/UNHCR, 2007a).

What are the Barriers to Education for IDP Children in Somaliland and Puntland?

To inform education programming for IDP children in Puntland, the Norwegian Refugee Council (NRC) carried out a study on household schooling choices among IDPs in Bossaso. Focus group discussions with IDP children and their mothers indicated that poverty is a key barrier to education for IDPs. There are an estimated 35,000 displaced persons living in 25 settlements in and around the town of Bossaso; about 60% are children under the age of 18 years (NRC, 2010).

The survey showed that most IDP households are poor and the majority face considerable constraints in feeding their families. Failure to meet education-related costs such as fees for tuition and school uniforms prevents poor families from sending their children to school. As a coping mechanism school-aged children are prevented from enrolling or forced to drop out of school due to their engagement in labor activities (NRC, 2010). In urban areas, IDP children contribute to the household economy by being engaged in income-generating activities. But also in rural households children play a significant part in household coping strategies. Younger children herd goats and sheep while older boys (*geel jire*) are herding camels (Cabdi, 2005; NRC,

2008). Their work is highly dependent on seasonal changes; during periods with little rainfall children walk longer distances or even relocate temporarily to watering points, which makes them miss school (NRC, 2008).

The predominant formal education system in Somalia does not adjust to seasonal attendance provoked by food shortages and drought-driven migration, nor does it adjust timetables to meet the needs of working children (Smith, 2007; NRC, 2008). IDP children are therefore vulnerable to long absences and so fall below the minimum amount of teaching time required to benefit from education.

Opportunity costs linked to education are another key barrier to education for IDPs (NRC, 2008; NRC, 2010). Opportunity costs refer to 'the result of the choice of going to school instead of – for example – performing tasks at home, made up by the loss of benefit a child could have achieved by contribution to household income through work' (UN, 2008: 3). When children are in school, families lose out on their contribution to the household economy, and a cost-benefit calculation at the household level often results in poor IDP families not enrolling their children or taking them out of school if opportunities for income-generating activities arise (NRC, 2010).

Due to the conflict, both Puntland and Somaliland have experienced a growing number of street children, especially in towns of Bosasso and Hargeisa. The majority, especially in Bosasso, are unaccompanied minors who got separated from their parents or guardians when they fled the conflict in the south. Without the clan safety net, they are increasingly at risk and less able to access their rights (Bradbury, 2008; NRC, 2010). Living on the streets without adult supervision, these children are vulnerable to sexual abuse, exploitative labor, drug abuse (*khat* chewing), military recruitment and criminal activities[3]. The street children remain extremely disadvantaged and have hardly any access to education or other social services (Cabdi, 2005; NRC, 2010).

It should be mentioned that displacement has also led to one unexpected benefit in education access, particularly for rural children. Education infra-structure is scarce in rural parts of Puntland and Somaliland, and does not adapt to the nomadic lifestyle of Somali pastoralists. But the majority of IDPs have moved into urban areas, and both Bossaso and Hargeisa have seen a steady flow of IDPs coming from the south, people fleeing from across the Ethiopian border and refugees returning from Ethiopia (Bradbury, 2008; NRC, 2008; NRC, 2010). Most adjust to an urban lifestyle and the shift from rural to urban living seems to have created better opportunities for education for the IDPs since they are now living in areas where access to basic services is comparatively better.

It is the national authority's duty to respect, protect and fulfill the right to education for internally displaced persons, and this duty should be reflected in national education laws, regulations and policies (INEE, 2010a). The Somaliland Ministry of Education categorize internally displaced children as 'disadvantaged and vulnerable children', but the education policy does not target this group in a systematic manner and assistance largely depends on the activities of NGO partners (Somaliland Ministry of Education, 2007a: 19). The Puntland Education Policy Paper (PEPP) also places strong emphasis on IDP education under the paragraph on 'Education for children of nomads and other disadvantaged groups', including focus on 'non-traditional methods of delivering education to nomadic communities/ IDPs (…)' (Puntland MOE, 2005: 7). Effective implementation of policies is lacking, and in line with the conclusions from UNESCO (2011) it can be argued that IDPs continue to be marginalized in their access to education in Puntland and Somaliland.

Challenges to Girl's Access to Education

More evident than the gap in education for displaced children in Puntland and Somaliland is the gender gap. Girls are disfavored at all levels of education, with disparity increasing with each additional grade in primary school. In Somaliland girls represent only 31% of enrolled children and below 30% for Puntland (EC, 2010; Somaliland MoE, 2007a). Research conducted by NRC (2008) among 29 households in IDP communities in Somaliland indicated that the opportunity cost involved in sending girls to school was a key reason why girls' participation in education is low, more than the actual costs related to schooling. The shift from rural to urban living and changing gender roles within the family has led to greater reliance on girls' and women's labor. Most women in urban IDP settlements are working hard to make ends meet with domestic tasks, casual employment or income-generating activities such as petty trade. When tasks become too demanding mothers will normally lean on their daughters for support, either by handing over domestic chores to daughters or engaging them in income-generating activities. In the choice between education and work, education will often loose (NRC, 2008, 2010).

Both girls and boys are involved in paid work which negatively affects their schooling: boys mainly work in the market while girls are engaged in household chores or work as domestic servants for better-off households. Girls earn far less than boys per month in the IDP settlements in Bosasso (between USD 15 – USD 22 for girls, and USD 31 – USD 46 for boys) (NRC, 2010) meaning that the opportunity cost of sending boys to school is higher than that of sending girls. Yet parents are more inclined to send their sons than their daughters to school.

The reluctance to sending girls to school despite their comparatively low contribution to household costs must be seen in relation to the value attributed to educating girls. According to the Quran education is not only a right but a duty for all females and males, and the Prophet Muhammad encouraged women to seek knowledge (UNICEF, 2002). Yet education for girls is given little value, since it is not considered relevant in preparation for adult life. As reflected in this Somali proverb, women's roles are closely linked to family life and Somali tradition discourages women from working outside the home: 'A mother's function is a cook, laundress, nurturer and wife to her husband' (Cabdi, 2005: 280). In NRC's Alternative Basic Education (ABE) programme, early marriage is one of the most common reasons given when girls drop out of school.

As gender roles are changing, more women are engaged in income-generating activities, and involvement in petty trade is considered acceptable (Cabdi, 2005). But even if education can prepare girls for working life, it will be subject to a cost-benefit analysis. Early marriage is common in Somali society, and after marriage the girl belongs to the family of her husband. Parents therefore consider that investing in girls' education will not benefit them: early marriage makes it unlikely that an employable daughter will make any financial contribution to her parents' home before marriage and therefore her earnings will mainly benefit her in-laws. So investment in education is not considered beneficial to the family (UNICEF, 2002; Cabdi, 2005; NRC, 2010).

Insecurity and fear of gender-based violence also prevents Somali girls from attending school. In NRC's IDP study, girls reported to have dropped out of school due to being harassed by youth groups in one of Hargeisa's largest IDP settlements. In rural areas parents also expressed concern about sending girls to school, since they had to walk long distances between school and home and there was widespread concern that girls would be subject to rape and violence (NRC, 2008).

More than 90% of Somali females undergo Female Genital Mutilation

(FGM), in most cases infibilation[4], which is normally performed on girls of school-going age (World Bank and UNFPA 2004). Limited research exists on the impact of FGM on girls' education, but there are indications of prolonged absence from school following the procedure. In NRC's study among IDPs in Somaliland, girls reported that FMG also has a long-term negative impact on their education since many experience problems passing menstrual discharge and are therefore absent from school during their monthly periods due to pain (NRC, 2008; NRC, 2010).

Girls' education is also hampered by the lack of a gender-responsive education system. In Somaliland only 16% of teachers are female; the number is 18% for Puntland (UNICEF, 2006). Lack of sex-segregated toilets and adequate water resources prevents girls' attendance. Several female respondents in NRC's study among IDP households reported that lack of adequate sanitary facilities made them not attend school during their menstrual periods. Stigma related to girls' maturity and their monthly periods also results in absence, especially if they do not have access to appropriate sanitary wear (NRC, 2008; INEE, 2010b).

Alternative Approaches to Narrowing the Education Gap

The authorities of Somaliland and Puntland have both made significant steps towards advancing education and clearly express their commitment to education for all in their education policies. Yet practical responses by the Government to address IDP education have been limited. When national authorities fail to fulfill the rights of IDPs, international humanitarian and development actors should play complementary roles (Brookings, 2010). This section elaborates on two initiatives by the Norwegian Refugee Council (NRC), aiming to fulfill the education rights of IDPs in Somaliland and Puntland with a particular emphasis on girls.

Alternative Basic Education in Somalia (ABE):

To fulfill the education rights of IDP children, and girls in particular, NRC started an alternative education programme in Somaliland in 2005 and in

Puntland and South-Central Somalia in 2007. Alternative education refers to 'all types of education programmes that are (…) not considered formal education' (Baxter & Bethke, 2009: 27). In response to the high number of over-age, out-of-school children, the Ministries of Education in Somaliland, Puntland and Somalia supported the development of an Alternative Basic Education (ABE) curriculum, with the assistance of international partners[5]. The ABE programme for the Somali context relies on an accelerated learning approach, where the Lower Primary curriculum (4 Grades) is condensed. This enables over-age learners to progress through the curriculum more rapidly than the formal learning path allows, and to enroll at Upper primary at a more age appropriate level. In Puntland and Somaliland, NRC targets out-of-school children aged 9/10 – 14[6].

The ABE program addresses many of the barriers limiting IDP children's access to education. NRC meets all monetary costs related to schooling (including provision of uniform and scholastic materials), but does not mitigate opportunity costs. Most ABE classes are held in formal schools where NRC has constructed additional classrooms or uses existing classrooms when they are not in use by other learners. The ABE curriculum was seen as relevant, making use of participatory methodologies and appropriate textbooks and teacher guides (Smith, 2007).

A key feature of alternative education is the ability to adjust to the daily and seasonal routines of learners. Where formal education is guided by national standards on length of the school year, terms and school days, alternative education may adjust to seasonal movement, harvest seasons, or extend the school year to allow completion of syllabus for learners in need. The fact that the ABE program is implemented in formal schools has made it difficult to operate with very flexible timetables, but most teaching happens during the afternoon shift when most working children have completed their responsibilities. When conflict or drought has disrupted education, or the accelerated rate of learning has made it difficult for learners to cope with the curriculum, the ABE cycle has been prolonged to allow for sufficient contact hours.

NRC placed strong emphasis on making ABE gender responsive. To address some of the cultural/traditional barriers to girls' education, NRC works closely with Community Education Committees (CECs) in mobilizing the community to support girls' education. In Somaliland a campaign on girls' right to education was carried out in all IDP communities where ABE is implemented, with the support of community and religious leaders. The campaign partly rested on the teachings of the Quran which are supportive of girls' education. Community sensitization by the CECs also included mobilization against the practice of FGM, though to a limited extent.

NRC addresses the 'gender gap' by having a clear enrollment policy stating that at least half of ABE learners should be female. The policy was supported by MOE and CECs and has been successful in facilitating equal access, though there are disparities in attendance and retention to the disfavor of girls. School feeding and 'take home' rations for girls provided by the World Food Programme contribute to improved attendance and improved wellbeing for children (EC, 2010). To motivate girls to attend schools during their monthly periods, sanitary kits are provided, composed of reusable sanitary pads, underwear and soap[7]. There has been limited systematic monitoring of the impact of the sanitary kits, but direct feedback from beneficiaries has been positive.

Initiatives have also been put in place by NRC to improve education quality and particularly the learning environment for girls. A policy of recruiting 40% female teachers is put in place. Though the target has not been met, the proportion of female teachers is significantly higher in ABE compared to formal schools. For instance, in Somaliland NRC had 36% female teachers in ABE compared to 11.9% in public schools (Somaliland MoE, 2007). NRC constructs education infrastructure to avoid congestion, including sex-segregated latrines. The organization has piloted the construction of gender-sensitive latrines with high walls in front of the entrance and sensitive placement in the school yard. Yet experiences from many ABE schools are that girls are reluctant to use the latrines, often due to lack of water (NRC, 2008). Training of ABE teachers, CEC members and Ministry of Education (MoE) inspectors and staff on gender-sensitive teaching approaches, monitoring and creating environments conducive to learning is also carried out to foster better education quality. In Somaliland a Code of Conduct for ABE teachers was developed due to the lack of a national code of conduct by the MOE, but later NRC and Save the Children supported the Ministry in developing an official Code of Conduct which is now being applied in formal and non-formal education (INEE & Skeie, 2008).

The ABE program had 80% retention rate of learners as an objective. Retention rates varied and a higher dropout rate was seen in areas affected by drought-driven migration, and among girls. A study comparing attendance in formal schools, integrated schools (Quranic and secular combined), *dugsis* and ABE in Bosasso indicated that ABE had the most regular attendance, without attributing it to specific initiatives (NRC, 2011).

In order to attempt to assess the quality of education provided through ABE, competency tests are administered to ABE leavers and formal Grade 4 leavers. Examinations from Somaliland showed that ABE learners performed slightly better than formal school pupils, and passing rates were also higher, 59% in ABE compared to 57% in formal schools (EC, 2010). In Puntland the competency tests show the opposite picture, where Grade 4 formal learners perform better than ABE learners (Puntland MoE, 2009). All in all the performance of ABE and formal school learners was quite balanced, despite the accelerated rate of learning in ABE, which puts heavy demands on learners.

Parallel to running the ABE program, NRC provided significant support to the Ministries of Education in Puntland and Somaliland, aiming at building the capacity of education authorities to provide education for disadvantaged groups. In partnership with Save the Children, NRC supported Somaliland MoE in the development of a National Strategy and Plan of Action for Female Participation in Education. The Puntland MoE was supported in the development of Inclusive Education guidelines, where great emphasis was placed on the use of alternative education to reach marginalized groups. Capacity building of MoE staff at national, regional and district level was also provided.

Conditional Voucher Programme in Puntland

To enable vulnerable ABE graduates to make the transit to Upper Primary formal school, NRC together with UNICEF initiated a pilot project in Puntland in 2009. The two-year project assisted 1000 vulnerable ABE leavers, including 600 girls, through a two-pronged approach: supporting education-related household costs and improving the quality of education in formal schools. Eighty per cent of beneficiaries were IDP households and the remaining 20% came from host communities.

The backbone of the pilot was a voucher system designed to alter the opportunity costs related to sending children to school. Vouchers '… provide access to pre-defined commodities or services. They can be exchanged in designated shops or in fairs and markets. The vouchers may be denominated either in cash, commodity or service value' (ECHO, 2009: 3). The vouchers were commodity-based and contained uniforms, scholastic materials, sanitary materials for girls and food items. Vouchers were conditional as learners had to commit to attending school regularly (85% of school days each month) and parents/guardians to refrain from engaging children in work that would negatively impact their education (Lodi, 2011). The second approach was to improve education quality in ten selected schools to which ABE learners moved on by providing teacher training, subsidizing schools' operational costs and upgrading school infrastructure.

The voucher pilot was an innovative approach to addressing education gaps, and there were no similar projects in Somalia to learn from. The NRC education team first did an assessment of education-related costs per household to decide on the value and content of vouchers. A market survey was conducted in Bosasso, assessing the availability of commodities needed by beneficiaries, the possible risk of inflation caused by the voucher project and beneficiaries' safe access to markets. It was concluded that Bosasso, with its busy harbor, could supply goods without fear of inflation, and that beneficiaries there have safe access to the markets at minimal costs. Preconditions for the selection of merchants were set, including the need to have a permanent shop in a target area (proximity to school and beneficiaries), sufficient capacity to deliver goods, have a regular license and be a taxpayer, and should not be affiliated with militia groups. Selected merchants were trained by NRC on the objective of the voucher approach and on the practicalities of the process: the invoice, methods of payment, the number of pupils and the name of the school served.

One thousand vulnerable families benefitted from the pilot project, including 20% host community children. All were sensitized about the objective of the project, and the conditionality of the vouchers. The mother/female guardian of the household was the receiver of the voucher and was responsible for ensuring that the conditionality was met.

The project was well received among beneficiaries and the vouchers were used as intended, to ensure participation in education for children from vulnerable households. The vouchers were commodity based with pre-agreed items, but there was some flexibility on quantities to allow households to make purchases based on their specific needs. On some occasions, particularly with foodstuff, more items were purchased than had been agreed, leaving less money to be spent on the other pre-defined goods.

An evaluation of the pilot project (August 2011) demonstrated that the project had achieved the main objectives of facilitating the transition of ABE learners to formal school, as well as their regular attendance and retention. The conditional voucher system was identified as a key reason for the success of the pilot project. Although the vouchers did not cover all education-related costs, nor fully subsidized opportunity costs, the provision of vouchers created commitment among IDP households to enroll and maintain their children in school. The project was particularly successful in its strategy to target girls, with 60% of beneficiaries being girls (Lodi, 2011). The availability of supplies in shops, very close supervision of the voucher scheme and monitoring children's participation in school by Community Education Committee members and NRC staff, and the fact that the voucher was managed by the mother/female guardian, are considered significant to ensuring the success of the pilot.

According to the external evaluation, the inclusion of 20% host community members also contributed to fostering local integration and mutual respect and understanding (Lodi, 2011). There were some requests from host community families to be included in the project. Strict selection criteria were set through a participatory process, involving NRC, CEC members and mothers from IDP communities. Broad ownership and the fact that participation in the project was vulnerability – based made it easier to justify decisions on whom to select. To avoid tension between IDPs and host communities the distribution of vouchers, which happened in schools, was often done on off-school days.

A ripple effect of the project was that it created a more positive perception of the IDPs among the host population, as IDPs were seen to represent an 'income' for the local merchants. The vouchers represented a steady income for the merchants, who were from the local communities. The merchants also expressed satisfaction with the capacity building they received by NRC's finance team as part of the project, including training on tendering and invoicing.

The pilot project only supported learners making the transit from ABE to formal school for the two first years after transition (Grade 5 and 6), and not the full 4-year Upper primary cycle. In other words, the project only managed to enhance transition and retention during the first two years, but did not necessarily improve completion. During the two years of support the project successfully enhanced retention. Dropout among the 1000 learners was only one per cent, which is significantly lower than the average in formal schools in Puntland, and for ABE learners who made the transit to formal school without support from the pilot project (Lodi, 2011).

A criticism from participants in the pilot was that the vouchers did not fully cover all education-related needs. That families still chose to keep their children in school shows that there is some commitment to investing in the education of their daughters and sons. Whether the pilot project has managed to create sufficient commitment to education so that families will invest in the two last years of formal education remains to be seen. There is also a question around defining the most effective value of the voucher, balancing the need to create incentive for education with the cost-efficiency of the project and the need not to create dependency.

Realizing Education For All for Somali Children: A Way Forward

Despite education for IDPs being a focus area in the education policies of Puntland and Somaliland, education assistance to this group is largely provided by non-government actors. Until the capacity of the education authorities to provide flexible education to disadvantaged groups is strengthened, and sufficient education sector budgets are ensured, NGOs will play an important part in ensuring education for specific groups. The ABE and Voucher projects are two examples among a range of NGO initiatives in Puntland and Somaliland. As NGOs continue to play an important role in education delivery, linkages with government policy and priorities become important in ensuring sustainability.

The involvement of the MoE in developing the ABE curriculum and implementation guidelines in Somaliland and Puntland has been important for the recognition of alternative education as a way of targeting disadvantaged groups. In partnership with ABE providers (NRC, Save the Children) the MoE is involved in the examination of ABE learners, including the administration of comparison tests between ABE leavers and Grade 4 leavers in formal schools.

The involvement of education authorities in providing ABE is enhanced by a gradual transfer of ABE teachers into the MoE teaching force. At the start of the project all ABE teachers were trained and paid by NRC, but monetary support from NRC was gradually reduced as the MoE took greater ownership. The non-formal ABE teachers were enrolled in an EC-funded teacher training program, providing in-service training to non-qualified teachers with the aim of certification. The majority of ABE teachers were certified to teach in the public system, which contributed significantly to increasing the female teaching force in Puntland and Somaliland.

The involvement of MoE in planning, implementation and evaluation of the ABE, and the transfer of experience and capacity (including teachers) to the education authorities, combined with capacity building of CECs to oversee ABE programs, contributed to a level of sustainability for the ABE. However, the overall sustainability of the voucher program is debatable. Clearly the programme has succeeded in moving on and retaining learners in school for two years after ABE graduation, but it is still unclear whether it has managed to foster sufficient commitment to education. The cut-off point for assistance has yet to be defined: what should be the minimum value of the vouchers and what is the minimum length of time that assistance should be provided?

According to the external evaluation there were indications that the voucher project had created changes in both communities and among education stakeholders. The Puntland Ministry of Education committed to take twenty teachers working in the ten supported schools onto the MoE payroll. The teachers were initially paid by the community. Puntland MoE also committed to providing all 1000 participating children with the necessary school materials. All merchants agreed to cover the costs of providing the school feed for one child during two years of formal education. Finally, and of great significance, the CEC committed to allowing 650 households to pay fifty per cent of school fees for the next two years and to waive fees for 247 extremely vulnerable children (Lodi, 2011). At the time of writing (November 2011) there is a discussion on how to continue the voucher project based on what has been learned from the pilot.

ABE and voucher programs are not a long-term solution, but in places like Puntland and Somaliland where the majority of children have missed out of school, they represent an important way of narrowing the education gap. A transitional approach where assistance is gradually phased out and responsibility handed over to education authorities seems to be the most sustainable approach. The capacity of MoE to deliver a wide range of formal and non-formal education must be built up, and since most NGO partners have limited capacity to support at the central strategic level, a coordinated approach to strengthening MoE's response strategies and policies is required. The ABE program was significant in creating acceptance for alternative education approaches, and the voucher project resulted in fewer financial burdens being placed on individual households by the MoE and in CECs agreeing to reduce payments. Both the ABE and the voucher project enabled internally displaced children, and especially girls, to fulfill their education rights.

> ## Questions for Further Discussion
>
> How can linkages between education and livelihoods assistance be created to better support the opportunity costs related to schooling? Should commitment to sending children, especially girls, to school be key targeting criteria for livelihoods programming?
>
> What are the long-term consequences of accelerated learning for the continued education of learners? Does the condensed curriculum and accelerated rate of learning prepare learners sufficiently to progress through education?
>
> What role should conditional voucher schemes play in education programming? There are limited experiences with using conditional vouchers for education and expanded knowledge on creation of dependency and sustainability is needed to inform programming.

Notes

1 NRC is an independent, humanitarian non-governmental organization which provides assistance and protection, and contributes towards durable solutions to refugees and internally displaced persons worldwide. One of NRC's core competencies is education in emergencies, and NRC has more than twenty years experience of providing education in conflict-affected countries, especially through non-formal education programmes. NRC has wide experience in running Accelerated Learning programmes in Africa.

2 The majority of IDPs are in south-central Somalia, and many have fled the capital Mogadishu for the Afgoye corridor, 10–30 kilometers to the north, making Afgoye probably the largest IDP settlement in the world (IDMC & RSC 2011).

3 IDP children in south-central Somalia are at risk of military recruitment, which has severe consequences for their protection and education. In March 2009, the UN Secretary-General reported that approximately 1300 children had been recruited into armed forces in Somalia. Most of the recruitment took place in schools (UNESCO 2010).

4 Infibulation (often referred to as Female Genital Mutilation Type III) refers to 'excision of part or all of the external genitalia and stitching/narrowing the vaginal opening' (World Bank & UNFPA 2004:17). In Galckayo it was reported that 100% of six- to eight-year-old girls who enrolled in school had been infibulated (ibid.).

5 ABE was first developed by Save the Children and the Ministry of Education in Somaliland to address the out-of-school children in Somaliland, and later the Norwegian Refugee Council (NRC) assisted the development of an accelerated curriculum for Puntland and for South Central Somalia. Thus there are three different accelerated curriculums for the Somali territory. In Somaliland, three levels of ABE correspond to the four grades of Lower primary education, while in Puntland two levels of ABE corresponds to the four grades of primary education.

6 The project is funded by the Norwegian Ministry of Foreign Affairs and the European Commission.

7 The kits were designed through focus group discussions with female teachers, local women and girls to ensure that locally acceptable materials and designed were used. The kits are provided to schoolgirls together with training by female teachers on how to use them.

References

Baxter, Pamela and Lynne Bethke (2009), *Alternative Education. Filling the gap in emergency and post-conflict situations. Education in Emergencies and Reconstruction.* Paris: IIEP, UNESCO and CfBT Education Trust.

Bradbury, Mark (2008), *Becoming Somaliland. African Issues.* London: Progressio.

Brophy, Michael and Emma Page (2007), 'Radio Literacy and Life Skills for Out-of-School Youth in Somalia. CICH Hiroshima University' in *Journal of International Cooperation in Education*, Vol. 10 No. 1 (2007), pp. 135–47. Hiroshima.

Brookings (2010), *IASC Framework on Durable Solutions for Internally Displaced Persons.* The Brookings Institution – University of Bern Project on Internal displacement. Bern: University of Bern.

Cabdi, Sucaad Ibrahim (2005), 'The impact of the war on the family' in: *Rebuilding Somaliland. Issues and Possibilities.* WSP International Somali Programme. Asmara: The Red Sea Press.

Danish Refugee Council (2007), *Profiling of Internally Displaced Persons. Process Documentation Report.* IDP Profiling Project Somalia.

Danish Refugee Council and UNHCR Branch office Somalia (2007a), *Report on profiling of Internally Displaced Persons Burco.* Final draft. IDP Profiling project Somaliland. Nairobi: DRC/UNHCR.

—(2007b), *Report on profiling of Internally Displaced Persons Bossaso.* Final draft. IDP Profiling Project Somalia. Nairobi: DRC/UNHCR.

ECHO (2009), *The use of Cash and Vouchers in Humanitarian Crisis.* DG ECHO funding guidelines. ec.europa.eu/echo/files/policies/sectoral/ECHO_Cash_Vouchers_Guidelines.pdf (Accessed 11 November 2011).

European Commission (June 2010), *Integrated Special Primary and Alternative Education (ISPABE). End Term Evaluation Report, final draft.* Submitted by: Rev. Grace Syong'oh. Nairobi: EC.

Internal Displacement Monitoring Centre (November 2010), *Learning in Displacement. Briefing paper on the right to education of internally displaced people.* Geneva: IDMC.

Internal Displacement Monitoring Centre (2011), *Internal Displacement: Global Overview of Trends and Development in 2010.* Geneva: IDMC/NRC.

Internal Displacement Monitoring Centre and Refugee Studies Centre (August 2011), *Unlocking protracted displacement. Somali Case study.* Working paper series no. 79. Oxford Department of International Development: University of Oxford. www.rsc.ox.ac.uk/publications/working-papers-folder_contents/RSCworkingpaper79.pdf/view (Accessed 9 November 2011).

Inter-Agency Network for Education in Emergencies (2008), *Case Study on the Implemtation of INEE Minimum Standards in Somaliland/Somalia.* Case study author: Silje Sjøvaag Skeie, Norwegian Refugee Council.

—(2010a), *Minimum Standards for Education: Preparedness, Response, Recovery.* New York: INEE/UNICEF.

—(2010b), *Gender Equality in and through education.* INEE Pocket Guide to Gender. Geneva: INEE.

Lodi, Camilla (August 2011), *Support to IDP Education and Pupils Transition from ABE to Formal School in Puntland. Project Evaluation.* Nairobi: NRC www.cashlearning.org/ (Accessed 31 October 2011).

Lewis, Ioan (2009), *Understanding Somalia and Somaliland. Culture, History, Society. 2nd impression 2009.* London: Hurst & Company.

Norwegian Refugee Council (December 2008), *Indigenous Perspectives on Girls' Education in Somaliland. Experience from NRC Supported School Communities.* Hargeisa: NRC. Unpublished.

—(August 2010), *Reaching out-of-school children through conditional cash transfers: A study on household schooling choices in Bossaso, Puntland, Somalia.* Author: Oscar Milafu Onam.

—(July 2011), *Increasing Access to Quality Education in Puntland: Lessons from Formal, Non-formal (ABE), Integrated Quranic Schools and Dugsi in Bosaso.* NRC: Unpublished .

Puntland Ministry of Education (2005), *Puntland Education Policy Paper. Final Draft.* Garowe: Puntland Ministry of Education.

—(December 2009), *Report for Competence Test between ABE level II leavers and Grade IV leavers in Puntland.* Garowe: Puntland Ministry of Education.

Smith, Dr. Harvey (2007), *'Formal' versus 'non-formal' basic education: prioritising alternative approaches in fragile states.* Oxford International Conference on Education and Development. September 2007. Thematic Section: 'Growing' education in difficult environments.

Somaliland Ministry of Education (2007a), *Education Sector Strategic Plan (2007 – 2011).* Final version, July 2007. Hargeisa: Ministry of Education, Republic of Somaliland.

—(2009), *ABE Examination report 22nd August.* Non-Formal Examination Unit. Somaliland National Examination and Certification Board. Hargeisa: Ministry of Education, Republic of Somaliland.

UN Committee on the Rights of the Child (2008), *The Right of the Child to Education in Emergency Situations.* www.crin.org/docs/08_Ad_hoc_group.pdf 16.11.2011. (Accessed 11 November 2011).

UNESCO (2011), *Education For All Global Monitoring Report 2011. The hidden crisis: Armed conflict and education.* Paris: UNESCO.

—(2010), *Education under Attack 2010.* Paris: UNESCO.

UNHCR (2011a), *Staggering Malnutrition rates as quarter of Somalia population uprooted. Briefing Notes,* 5 July 2011. Geneva: UNHCR www.unhcr.org/4e12f1f36.html Accessed (October 2011).

UNHCR Somalia (April 2011b), *Total IDPs.* ochaonline.un.org/somalia/MapCentre/ThematicMaps/tabid/2724/language/en-US/Default.aspx#idps (Accessed November 2011).

UNHCR (15.10.2011), *Somalis in the East and Horn of Africa Region Update* www.unhcr.org/4e8c56919.pdf (Accessed) (October 2011).

UNICEF (2002), *Women's rights in Islam and Somali Culture.* Hargeysa, Somaliland: UNICEF, The Academy for Peace and Development www.unicef.org/somalia/SOM_WomenInIslam.pdf

—(2007), *Primary Education survey Somalia 2006/2007.* Draft 3. Nairobi: UNICEF.

UNOCHA (2004), *Guiding Principles on Internal Displacement. Second Edition.* Bern: Brookings Institute/UN.

World Bank and UNFPA (2004), *Female Genital Mutilation/Cutting in Somalia.* siteresources.worldbank.org/INTSOMALIA/Data%20and%20Reference/20316684/FGM_Final_Report.pdf (Accessed November 2011).

The Hidden Crisis: Armed Conflict and Education

Kevin Watkins

3

Chapter Outline

Abstract

This chapter draws on the 2011 UNESCO Education for All Global Monitoring Report which highlighted the alarming fact that 'armed conflict is robbing 28 million children of an education'. The author, who led the team which produced the report, examines the impact of conflict on education. He focuses in particular on the distinctive problems faced by IDPs and the systematic failure of national governments and the international community to address their needs. While the primary responsibility to protect and assist IDPs lies with national authorities, that responsibility is seldom discharged, and in some cases governments are directly implicated in violating the rights of IDPs to an education. The international response to the challenge posed by armed conflict suffers from chronic under-financing, short-termism, an aid architecture that is unfit for purpose and – critically – weak political leadership. These failures are not only robbing displaced children of their right to education, but undermining the potential role of education as a force for peace, social reconstruction and economic recovery in ethnically and linguistically diverse societies seeking to escape the vicious circle of armed conflict and underdevelopment.

Introduction

Civil war has been described as 'development in reverse' (Collier 2007). Even short episodes of violent conflict can slow or reverse social and economic gains built up over generations, with devastating consequences for human development. The underlying dynamics and transmission mechanisms linking conflict and international development are widely debated. Some commentators emphasize the economic forces that limit opportunity, weaken economic growth, and create incentives for young people to engage in rebellion (Collier and Hoeffler, 2004; Collier 2007). Others focus on a wider set of grievances associated with inequality and ethnic fragmentation (Østby, 2008; Stewart, 2010). There is less room for debate over the consequences of war. Developing countries affected by armed conflict are characterized by slow growth and low levels of human development. These countries dominate the lower reaches of the global league table for indicators ranging from child survival to nutrition, literacy and poverty. Most are making slow progress towards the 2015 Millennium development Goals (MDGs). In 2011 the United Nations issued a stark warning that 'armed conflict remains a major threat to human security and to hard-won MDGs' (United Nations, 2010: 4). It is increasingly clear that failure to address the special needs of conflict-affected countries will leave the world far short of the 2015 development targets. Within the broader set of countries categorized by the World Bank as 'fragile states', there is a growing recognition that those affected by armed conflict pose distinctive challenges (World Bank, 2011). Yet effective responses to the challenges remain elusive.

Nowhere is the impact of civil war more painfully apparent than in education. UNESCO's 2011 *Education for All Global Monitoring Report* drew attention to what it described as a 'hidden crisis' in the education systems of conflict-affected states. It documented the chilling effects of what has become one of the defining features of many conflicts: namely, the deliberate targeting of civilians and civilian infrastructure. From Afghanistan to Pakistan, to Yemen, South Sudan and the Democratic Republic of Congo, schoolchildren, teachers and classrooms have been deliberately targeted by armed factions. The problem is not that education is getting caught in the cross-fire but that children and education systems are seen as legitimate targets. Beyond the immediate humanitarian impacts, the 'hidden crisis' in education has far-reaching consequences. In an increasingly knowledge-based global economy, the destruction of opportunities for learning in many of the world's poorest countries will undermine prospects for economic growth, employment creation, poverty reduction and the achievement of wider development goals.

This chapter draws on the analysis of the 2011 Global Monitoring Report. It is divided into three sections. The first documents the state of education in conflict-affected states. Section two looks at the distinctive problems facing internally displaced people (IDPs) – and at the systemic failure of national governments and the international community to address these problems. Section three sets out a broad agenda for reform, highlighting the need for new approaches to the provision of education in conflict-affected states.

The Impact of Armed Conflict on Education

Isolating the effects of armed conflict on education is not straightforward. National conflicts vary in their geographic spread, duration and intensity. Moreover, the correlation between armed conflict on the one side and high levels of deprivation in education on the other has to be treated with caution – association is not in itself evidence of causation. Many of the mechanisms linking civil wars to education are indirect and hard to measure. Damage to school infrastructure is easy to document in principle, though UN agencies have largely shunned their responsibility to monitor and report on this issue (O'Malley, 2010a). It is far more difficult to assess the impact of psychological trauma among children affected by war, or the degree to which financial resources are being diverted from spending on education to pay for military hardware.

Even the task of identifying a distinctive group of conflict-affected states is problematic. By their very nature, the thresholds and standard measurement indicators – such as battlefield casualties and civilian deaths – used to identify conflicts include arbitrary judgements. Simple binary categories such as 'conflict-affected' and 'non-conflict-affected' may have an obvious appeal for researchers seeking to construct econometric modelling exercises. They are of considerably less value in making sense of a non-binary world in which countries slip in and out of conflict, and where the lines between different forms of conflict are blurred.

Using data from the Peace Research Institute Oslo (PRIO) and the Uppsala Conflict data program (UCPD), the UNESCO report identified thirty low and lower-middle income countries affected by conflict between 1999 and 2008. Collectively, these countries experienced forty-three episodes of violent conflict with an average duration of twelve years in the low-income states and twenty-two years in lower-middle-income states (UNESCO, 2011a: 138). The data used in the UNESCO survey illustrate the difficulties involved in cross-country comparison. On the PRIO definition India is a conflict-affected state along with countries such as the Democratic Republic of Congo, even though the scale, intensity and impact of the conflicts are clearly very different. Similarly, Mexico is not included in the list because the country does not meet the criteria for 'contested incompatibility' over territory and government authority, even though narcotic-related violence in 2010 claimed more lives than the war in Afghanistan.

With all the caveats about data and causality in mind, what is the state of education in conflict-affected states? Headline numbers tell their own story. As a group, the thirty developing countries affected by conflict account for one-quarter of the world's primary school-age children, but almost half of all children in that age group – around 28 million in total – who are out of school (UNESCO, 2011a). The deficit extends beyond primary school. Gross enrolment rates in secondary education in the conflict-affected countries are 30% lower than the average for countries not affected by conflict. Gender gaps are also far wider (2011a: 132). Girls in conflict-affected states are around ten per cent less likely to be in primary school and 20% less likely to be in secondary school.

To add to an already bleak picture, school indicators do not capture wider impacts with a very direct bearing on education. Extreme malnutrition in the early years before children enter school impairs cognitive development, with damaging and largely irreversible consequences for learning achievement in the school years. Living in a conflict-affected state doubles the risk of children not surviving to their fifth birthday – an outcome that reflects the combined effect of malnutrition and limited access to basic health services (UNESCO, 2011a: 133). The incidence of moderate and severe stunting, the most sensitive early childhood nutrition indicator, is twice as high – around 38% – in conflict-affected states as in other developing countries. Adult literacy, one of the strongest predictors for school attendance and learning achievement, is also far lower in countries experiencing armed conflict (2011a: 133).

National data can obscure the sub-national impacts of conflict on education. These impacts are important because armed violence is typically spread very unevenly across different regions. To take an extreme case, the armed rebellion violence in the Indian state of Chattisgarh has a minimal impact on national school enrolment and is highly localized even within the state. At the other end of the spectrum, the deadly spiral of violence in the Democratic Republic of Congo is highly concentrated in the eastern region of the country.

Household survey data and national census documents provide an insight into the localized effects of conflict on education. Using the Deprivation and Marginalization in Education (DME) database, which draws on these sources, the 2011 UNESCO report documented a range of sub-national impacts. Consider first the case of North Kivu, in eastern Democratic Republic of Congo (2011a: 134). Around one-third of young people aged 17–22 in the province have received less than two years in education. That figure is around twice the national average. The data analysis also reveals marked wealth and gender effects. Fewer than 15% of males from wealthy households covered in the survey received less than two years of education, compared to almost half of females from poor households. There are many complex factors behind these outcomes. However, the disaggregated household data provide circum-stantial evidence that the very high levels of gender-based violence and loss of assets among households characterized by high levels of poverty have left a very deep imprint on the distribution of opportunities for education in North Kivu. In the first half of 2009 alone, military operations in the Kivu provinces resulted in reports of more than 1,400 civilian deaths and 7,500 rapes.

While eastern Democratic Republic of Congo is an extreme case it is also a microcosm of early twenty-first century conflict. Across the world's poorest countries, armed groups, including state actors, have systematically targeted civilians and civilian infrastructure. At a superficial level, this is evident from the casualty profiles associated with major conflicts. Estimates for the Democratic Republic of Congo put the 'excess death' toll resulting from hunger and disease at over five million (Coghlan et al., 2008). The equivalent figure for South Sudan has been put at over two million (Guha-Sapir, 2005).

Behind these figures are military strategies geared not towards engagement with other armed groups but the destruction of livelihoods, violations of human rights and the imposition of terror on civilian populations. In a few cases those responsible have been charged with war crimes. The most prominent indicted war criminal still at large is President al-Bashir of Sudan, who is accused of ordering the killing, rape and displacement of civilian populations in Darfur. But in some respects his and other well-publicised cases have deflected attention from the widespread and routine attacks on civilians reported through the United Nations elaborate (though, it has to be said, largely ineffective) mechanisms for monitoring such attacks. Many of these attacks deliberately target children and schools as part of a wider 'war against civilians' (O'Malley, 2010b; UNESCO, 2011a).

The displacement of civilian populations is both an intended and unintended consequence of armed groups engaged in conflict. Patterns of displacement vary across countries and reflect the underlying drivers of localized conflicts. Episodes from late 2011 and early 2012 illustrate the ongoing scale of displacement (IDMC, 2012). In northern Nigeria the mass displacement of (mainly Christian) ethnic Igbo people in the face of threats from militants of the Boko Haram movement was matched by the counterpart displacement of (mainly Muslim) Yoruba people in the southern state of Benin. In South Sudan, clashes between Nuer and Murle people resulted in the displacement of over 60,000 people amidst widespread killing. Inevitably, education systems are affected by episodes such as these. In northern Kenya, the education of over 3,000 children was disrupted in Moyale county, which borders Ethiopia, following clashes between rival herding communities which resulted in the closure of seventeen schools.

With 27.5 million IDPs as of December 2010 – an increase of around half a million over the previous year, the scale of displacement presents a challenge to both national governments and the international community. Nowhere is that challenge greater than in Sudan. Before the independence of South Sudan, the national IDP figure stood at between 4.5 million and 5.2 million – one of the highest levels in the world (IDMC, 2011a: 53). Many of these people are now returning from IDP camps around Khartoum and other cities in the North to build a future in South Sudan. The Democratic Republic of Congo has an IDP population estimated at 1.7 million (IDMC, 2011a: 45). While the government and some donors maintain the fiction that the country now merits post-conflict status, at least 400,000 people were newly displaced in 2010. Even before the food crisis and upsurge in violence in Somalia, at least 300,000 people were displaced. Outside Africa, the countries with the largest IDP populations are Colombia (over 3.6 million), Iraq and Pakistan, where almost one million people are still displaced as a result of the conflict in the north-west. In January 2011 a reported 309,000 people were still displaced in Afghanistan as a result of armed conflict, generalized violence and human rights abuses – higher than at any time since 2005 (IDMC, 2011b: 5).

Global statistics such as these provide a static snapshot of what is often a fast-moving picture. During 2010 almost three million people were newly displaced as a result of armed conflict, while 2.1 million returned to their homes (IDMC, 2011a). As these figures suggest there is sometimes a great deal of flux in the IDP population. People may be forced out of their homes, or leave on a precautionary basis, for short periods. In other cases, they may leave for many years. This unpredictability adds to the complexity of compiling and assessing statistics, as does the location of IDPs. While some relocate to formal camps, most live in the midst of host communities, making it difficult to identify a distinctive population. All of these factors complicate the task of assessing IDP education needs and providing basic services.

For all these uncertainties there is no room for doubt over the scale of the problems faced by IDPs. Physical displacement has profound consequences for education because it uproots communities and separates children from their schools, teachers and home environment. The sheer size of this population makes the state of education among IDP children a matter of the utmost importance for human development and progress towards the MDGs. These children almost certainly represent a very large share of the out-of-school numbers in conflict-affected areas. They face elevated risks of stunting and childhood mortality. Yet evidence on the state of education and well-being among IDP children is woefully inadequate.

This is part of a wider information deficit (IDMC, 2011a). Few national authorities demonstrate a serious commitment to the collection of information on displaced populations. While many international agencies – including UNICEF and UNHCR – and non-government organizations are involved in humanitarian and development work with IDPs, they typically apply different methodologies in data collection. Some of the biggest data gaps surround IDPs in protracted displacement. These issues matter because in the absence of information it is difficult to estimate either the costs of providing services, or the characteristics of people – their age profile, income levels, education and health status – needing support.

Getting By and Going Without – Education for IDPs

The provision of education is of critical importance for displaced children. Going to school can provide a sense of normality, a safe space and psychological support. Classrooms can offer a safe haven in the world of a child whose life has been turned upside down by armed conflict. Beyond the immediate benefits, education equips children with the opportunity to acquire a human capital asset which they can carry with them. For those subjected to repeat or long-term displacement, protracted periods out of school raise the spectre of a lifetime disadvantage. While the difficulty of maintaining education in conflict situations is self-evident, displaced children cannot afford to wait until conflicts end to exercise their right to education.

Across the world's conflict-affected regions, IDP parents make extraordinary efforts to keep alive opportunities for education. In a number of countries including the Democratic Republic of Congo, displaced communities operate 'bush schools' in forests, using volunteer teachers to provide lessons (IRIN, 2010). The author has witnessed at first hand the resilience and innovation of IDPs in maintaining access to schooling, however rudimentary (Watkins, 2011). In a visit to one camp for IDPs in Kachange district, in the Democratic Republic of Congo's North Kivu province, displaced people had built their own school and hired a local teacher. Many children were helping to pay for their education by working as charcoal sellers after school. In the Swat valley area of Pakistan, communities displaced by the violence which occurred in 2008 and 2009 created makeshift schools in camps and ruined buildings (UNESCO, 2011a: 200).

For all these efforts, many IDPs fight a losing battle to secure an education for their children. While global data is lacking, there is no shortage of research documenting serious shortfalls. One study of three districts in the Khyber Pakhtunkhwa region of Pakistan found evidence that upwards of 600,000 children had missed one or more years of schooling as a result of conflict (Ferris and Winthrop, 2010). In rural areas of North Kivu province, Democratic Republic of Congo, only around one-third of children had access to basic education in 2009 (IDMC, 2009). In Yemen, access to basic education is very limited for at least 55,000 displaced children, many of whom have missed up to two years of school as a result of violence (IDMC, 2010). Even when there is some provision of education, opportunities are often severely circumscribed. One 2008 survey of IDP communities in North and West Darfur found that primary schools were available and accessible. However, only half the school provided instruction across all eight grades of the basic education cycle and pupil-teacher ratios in excess of 50:1 were the norm (Lloyd et al., 2010).

The education barriers facing IDP children vary across countries. Cost is one of the highest barriers. Having lost their assets and savings and seen their livelihoods disrupted, IDP parents are seldom in a position to pay primary school fees. The absence of a functioning public education system can exacerbate the problem. Across eastern Democratic Republic of Congo education provision and finance is largely privatized, with schools provided by churches and non-government organizations and costs met out of the pockets of parents. In 2008 fees of US$5 per term were sufficient to exclude many IDP children (OCHA, 2010; Bailey, 2009). Similar outcomes have been reported for countries as diverse as Chad, Yemen, Somalia and Afghanistan (IDMC, 2010).

The experience of South Sudan is instructive because it draws attention to wider concerns (UNESCO, 2011b). Many millions of IDPs are now returning from IDP camps in the North and from refugee camps in neighbouring countries. Returnees place a high premium on education. Yet their children face grim prospects, especially if they are female. With a primary net enrolment rate of just 44% (the second lowest in the world) there are some 1.3 million primary school age children out of school (2011b: 6). The enrolment rate for secondary education – four per cent – is the lowest in the world. Gender gaps are among the widest reported through the international system. In 2010, there were just seven girls for every ten boys in primary school, and reportedly only 400 girls in the last grade of secondary school (2011b: 1). The new country has chronic shortages of qualified teachers, classrooms and books. Apart from all of these shortages, the Government of South Sudan is struggling to integrate children returning from IDP camps in the North, where Arabic was the medium of instruction (2011b: 18).

Despite a national policy of providing free basic education, the costs involved in attending school are still unaffordable for many families. One detailed study in Yei, the second largest urban centre in Central Equatoria, found that 'school fees were widely reported to be the main constraint to accessing education' (Martin and Sluga, 2011: 19). The fees encompassed both formal charges, which rose or fell depending on government transfers to schools, and a wide range of additional charges (for books, uniforms and informal fees). Financial pressures upon households often forced parents to make choices about which child to educate. With a strong gender preference in favour of investing in a boy's education, this appears to have reinforced gender inequalities. Moreover, many of the children returning to Yei are at a considerable disadvantage because they started their education in Arabic-language IDP camps. They therefore face the dual challenge of learning to read, write and speak English, as well as the local Kakwa language (2011: 20).

Other barriers to IDP education loom very large. In some contexts, insecurity is a major concern. Recent evidence from eastern Democratic Republic of Congo has shown that several militia, including those linked to government forces, continue forcibly to recruit children from IDP populations (IDMC, 2011c). Alongside the threat of rape and sexual violence, this creates obvious disincentives against parents sending their children to school. IDP children also face the same problems as many other children in conflict-affected areas. For example, there are some emergencies in which schools have either been used for military purposes (as in Yemen) or to house a displaced population (as in Pakistan). When opportunities to return home arise, governments often fail to create the conditions for the restoration of basic services. In Uganda, a whole generation of displaced children in the northern part of the country has been denied access to decent quality basic education and there has been insufficient planning and resourcing for the re-opening of schools in the villages to which children are returning (IDMC, 2011a).

National planning rules represent another barrier in some countries. Many of the refugees returning to Afghanistan have joined IDPs in informal settlements around Kabul, the capital city. In 2010 there were an estimated 30 slum settlements hosting people displaced by conflict. Most of the land on which these settlements are based belongs to the government, which has been reluctant to provide the formal residency entitlements that would allow people to claim basic services.

While the conflicts which generate IDPs are local and national the international architecture for providing support is weak and ineffective. Unlike refugees, who are covered by a legal framework – the 1951 United Nations Convention relating to the Status of Refugees – which establishes internationally accepted norms, rights and entitlements, along with an international agency (UNHCR) mandated to protect their interests and hold governments to account, there is no legally binding instrument upholding the rights of IDPs (Ferris and Winthrop, 2010). Responsibility for protecting and assisting IDPs rests with national authorities. In countries where the same authorities are implicated in violating the rights of IDPs, or where government lacks the resources, capacity or political will to provide security and basic services, this is obviously problematic. The legal and normative vacuum has some very direct consequences for education.

The international aid architecture

International aid practices relating to education for displaced children leave a great deal to be desired. Education suffers from a triple disadvantage: it receives a small fraction of humanitarian aid; only a small share of the aid requested is delivered; and aid priorities are often skewed by donor strategic interests, with damaging consequences for some of the world's poorest countries.

Most of the aid directed towards conflict-affected states that are home to IDPs is channelled through the humanitarian aid system. The share of humanitarian assistance in overall aid has climbed steadily over the past decade, from 7% in 2000 to 12% – or around $12bn – in 2008. Conflict-affected states account for around three-quarters of this aid. However, the distribution of aid that flows to these states is heavily influenced by the foreign policy goals of donors. In 2007 and 2008 Afghanistan received more aid than the combined total for the Democratic Republic of Congo and Sudan, while Iraq received over twice their combined total (OECD-DAC, 2010).

Education is not a priority in the humanitarian aid system. It accounts for just around two per cent of the development assistance envelope. To make matters worse, the education sector receives the smallest share of the aid requested through humanitarian aid appeals. Looking across the consolidated aid appeals for all sectors, an average of 72% of requests were met, compared to just 38% for education (UNESCO, 2011a: 205). In the case of the Central Emergency Response Fund, a pooled multilateral resource, education has received just 1.3% of the resources allocated since its foundation in 2006 (2011a: 205). Here too, strategic considerations weigh heavily in aid allocation. In Afghanistan, education has been seen as a central part of the wider reconstruction efforts. In 2007–8, aid to the sector averaged US$120m. Over the same period, Sudan received just US$38 million, while Chad, Côte d'Ivoire and Somalia received a combined total of just over US$20m.

While aid agencies constantly stress the importance of working across the 'humanitarian-development divide', when it comes to education the divide is firmly in place. Given that humanitarian aid accounts for the lion's share of development assistance to conflict-affected states, one consequence of the divide is that limited external support is available for IDP education. Unfortunately, the data on the share of education in humanitarian aid and appeals funded tell just part of the story. The requests that are put forward through consolidated humanitarian appeals are constructed through partnerships of donors and non-government organizations – known as 'clusters' – which come together in an exercise ostensibly aimed at identifying the needs of IDPs. In reality, the requests for education are almost entirely delinked from credible needs-based assessment exercises.

Even a schematic glance across some of the recent consolidated appeals documents captures the problem (UNESCO, 2011a: 207). In the case of North Kivu in the Democratic Republic of Congo, the 'education cluster' submitted a request in 2010 for $25m to support IDP education. This was in a context where the IDP population was estimated at almost two million, and where only around one-third of children enjoyed access to basic education. In the event, just US$3.6 million had been funded by mid-year. In the same year, the 'education cluster' request for Pakistan amounted to US$30m to address the needs of an estimated two million displaced children. Less than one-fifth of this amount had been funded by mid-year.

Chronic under-financing is compounded by equally chronic short-termism. Unlike some natural humanitarian emergencies – such as those associated with floods and earthquakes – those in education are often both predictable and long-term. As already noted the average duration of an armed conflict in a low-income country is twelve years (and almost double that in lower middle-income countries). An effective response to the needs of IDPs, especially in a sector like education, requires predictable, long-term financing.

That is not how the humanitarian aid system operates. Appeals processes are geared towards annual budget cycles, with funding levels heavily influenced by the vagaries of international appeal processes. When refugee camps serving Somalis in northern Kenya are faced with a surge in new arrivals, as they were during the conflict and food security crisis in 2011, UNHCR has to respond by launching appeals. One consequence has been its failure to maintain education provision in the face of rising needs (UNESCO, 2011a; Rose, 2010). In north-eastern Democratic Republic of Congo major international non-government organizations are frequently forced to finance long-term education interventions with short-term humanitarian aid, often with predictably unfortunate consequences. Save the Children, a UK-based non-government organization, has been forced to scale-back on programs in the face of donor reluctance to sustain support. Another problem facing such agencies is the very high transaction costs associated with applications for large numbers of small grants from humanitarian agencies (Dolan and Ndaruhutse, 2010).

Strategies for Reform

Armed conflict represents one of the great human development challenges of the twenty-first century. The United Nations architecture created to protect human rights and promote peace in the wake of conflicts of the twentieth century is no longer fit for purpose. The previous Secretary General of the United Nations recognized this and set out an agenda for reform encompassing strengthened provisions for the protection of human rights, conflict-prevention, reconstruction and peace-building (UN, 2005). But the political momentum behind a strengthened role for the UN remains limited. Along with the wider multilateral system, the UN has suffered a crisis of legitimacy and credibility as a result of what many countries see as the unilateralism, double standards and selective approach to the protection of human rights applied by western governments. Changing this picture is vital if the problems identified in this chapter are to be addressed.

The protection of children and education systems should be a rallying point for reform of the UN. The best form of protection in this case is to prevent displacement, not action after the event. While this is an issue that goes beyond the scope of the current chapter, the human rights architecture for protecting children and education is unbalanced. The UN conducts extensive monitoring of human rights abuses against children, including sexual violence, and the 2011 decision of the Security Council to make attacks on schools a trigger for investigation under the Monitoring and Reporting Mechanism marks a welcome addition to the remit. However, if monitoring is to be effective it has be backed by effective sanctions against persistent and egregious offenders, including governments that fail to counter the prevailing culture of impunity. Sanctions may be a blunt instrument in some respects. But under the right conditions – including the prospect of prosecution by the International Criminal Court – they can create powerful disincentive and deterrent effects against the acts of terror that fuel displacement. Those conditions do not currently exist (UNESCO, 2011a).

Strengthening the entitlements of IDPs to education will require a wide range of national and international policy interventions. Very few countries have effective and accessible processes in place to provide legal backing or redress to displaced people. The restitution of property and compensation for loss of assets can facilitate return and other settlement options, with attendant benefits for education. Yet while several countries – including Afghanistan, Côte d'Ivoire and Uganda – have introduced legislation in this area, few have implemented meaningful reform. This reinforces what might be termed the 'legal invisibility' of IDPs. Although there are at least fifty countries with IDP populations, only eighteen include references to IDPs in national laws and policies (Ferris, 2010a; Ferris and Winthrop, 2010). In the case of education, the interface between national and international provision reinforces the difficulties facing IDPs. While the international Guiding Principles affirm the right of IDPs to receive an education 'which shall be free and compulsory at the primary level', the guidelines are not legally binding on governments.

There are alternatives. In Colombia, which has one of the world's largest IDP populations, the Constitutional Court issued a ruling in 2004 which determined that government was failing to discharge its obligations to IDPs. The result was a national strategy for strengthening IDP rights and entitlements, overseen by a new agency – the national system for Attention to the Displaced Population – working across all ministries. Education was identified as a priority area. Under Colombian law, displaced children are now automatically eligible for free education, and schools must accept pupils without requiring previous proof of education (Ferris, 2010b; Birkenes, 2006; Cepeda Espinosa, 2009).

Sub-Saharan Africa is the one region in which governments have come together to address the IDP issue. The International Conference on the Great Lakes in 2006 resulted in eleven states signing the Pact on Security, Stability and Development. The Pact was the first multilateral mechanism to impose legal obligations on governments to protect the rights of IDPs. This was followed in 2009 by the Africa union's adoption of the Convention for the Protection and Assistance of Internally Displaced persons in Africa – the Kampala Convention. The Convention, which was negotiated over five years, covers the entire region and includes provisions requiring governments to deliver basic services, including education. Unfortunately, delivery has been less impressive than content. The provisions of the Great Lakes Pact have not been enacted in national legislation, while the Kampala Convention will only come into force once it has been ratified by fifteen countries.

National legislative action to secure IDP entitlements to education is critical. Without an enabling legislative environment, the principles and decrees adopted by governments carry little weight on the ground. The IDP provisions in Colombian law and the Kampala Convention provide effective blueprints that could be adapted. Alongside this process of establishing rights, authorities have to determine needs. That means stepping up efforts to collect data and develop more comprehensive information systems on displaced populations.

Given the constrained budget circumstances of many poor countries with large IDP populations, international aid has a vital role to play in addressing problems in education and other areas. This will require a shift in what has become an outmoded and anachronistic humanitarian mindset. IDPs caught up in conflict demonstrate through their own actions that they view education as a priority. The extraordinary efforts they make to get their children into school speaks volumes about their commitment and ambition. By contrast, humanitarian aid agencies and non-government agencies continue to see education as a peripheral issue, as reflected by the miniscule share of emergency assistance allocated to education. Without downplaying the significance of meeting priority needs in other areas – including food, clean water, shelter and health – the limited place of education in humanitarian provision bears the hallmarks of a system that is unresponsive to local needs and unaccountable to IDPs caught up in conflict.

More effective aid for education will also require new approaches to needs assessment and budgeting. The humanitarian cluster system through which donors, UN agencies and non-government organizations assess needs, estimate financing requirements and make requests for humanitarian support has a mixed record. Education was a late entrant to the system, and the education cluster has strengthened coordination. Yet the agencies involved have not developed a credible system for needs assessment. Nor have they engineered an approach for translating needs into financing requests. In many respects, the term 'needs assessment' is a misnomer in the case of education. For the most part, the agencies involved assess their own capacity for scaling-up aid through existing projects, taking into account their own assessment of the likely financing envelope. This is an area in which the major UN agencies with a responsibility in education – UNESCO, UNICEF and, to a lesser degree, UNHCR – should come together to conduct regular and more robust IDP needs assessments.

Even the best assessments and the most robust data will be of little value in the absence of reforms to the humanitarian aid architecture. Some conflicts share the characteristics of natural emergencies. They occur as short, sharp and intensive periods of disruption. However, most armed conflicts are long-running, intermittent and uneven in their effects, and they require flexible but predictable financing responses. Against this backdrop, donors should consider scaling up pooled funds for humanitarian aid, such as the Central

Emergency Response Fund (which received US$400m in 2009) and the Common Humanitarian Fund (US$330m in 2009) and setting aside a fixed share of around ten per cent for education (Development Initiatives 2010a).

Current aid practices and responses to countries affected by armed conflict suffer from a widespread 'binary world syndrome' in the donor community. Most aid agencies tend to view aid recipients either as conflict-affected, and hence subjects for humanitarian support, or as stable development partners ready for long-term aid commitments. Reality is more prosaic – and it requires a more flexible response.

The South Sudan case provides a useful lesson. Some six years have now passed since a comprehensive peace accord brought to an end the long-running civil war. Yet over 80% of aid to South Sudan takes the form of humanitarian development assistance, most of it short-term. Donors have yet to put in place a comprehensive financing strategy for supporting reconstruction in education. South Sudan has received no support from the Global Partnership for Education, the principle multilateral facility for education aid which operates under the auspices of the World Bank. Moreover, the major pooled fund created after the peace settlement to support reconstruction – the Multi-Donor Trust Fund – registered an exceptionally low rate of disbursement. By 2009, donors had paid in US$520m but less than one-half had been allocated (MDTF for Southern Sudan, 2010: 17). Education was one of the worst affected sectors, with just over one third of allocated funds disbursed by the end of 2009. The World Bank, which administered the MDTF, attributed responsibility for the slow disbursement to the Government of South Sudan, claiming that its ministries were unable to meet performance and accountability requirements (2010: 18). Given the self-evident and highly predictable capacity constraints facing the Government of South Sudan, the lack of flexibility demonstrated by the World Bank raises questions about its wider relevance to conflict-affected states. But the net effect of its actions – or, more accurately in this context, inactions – was that money which could have been used to build schools, buy textbooks and get children into school, remained locked in bank accounts (UNESCO, 2011; Foster et al., 2010; MDTF, for Southern Sudan, 2010).

Delayed support for reconstruction in education has come at a high price for South Sudan. Many children now out-of-school might have been in school had donors moved more decisively. Moreover, decisive action in education could have helped to underpin a fragile peace, providing hope and opportunities to returning IDPs and the wider population. In the event, many

IDPs are returning to South Sudan with high expectations and aspirations for their children, only to resettle in villages lacking schools and teachers. The loss of a potential peace dividend goes beyond access to education. Today the greatest threats to peace and security for most people in South Sudan come not from an aggressive neighbor in the North, but from long-standing rivalries and competition linked to group identity. The education system is an institution, perhaps the only institution in the country, with the potential to instill in children a sense of shared national identity, alongside a shared recognition and respect for the different ethnic groups that make up South Sudan. Underpinning the peace with the development of a school curriculum, textbook and teacher-training programs could have counteracted the centrifugal ethnic forces that fuel ethnic violence and threaten to weaken the fabric of the new country. The opportunity is still there – but far more decisive action is needed.

The experience of South Sudan underscores the critical place of reconstruction and peace-building in education. Transitions from armed-conflict to peace are seldom smooth. All too often countries emerge from episodes of violence, only to slip back into war. Donor caution is part of the problem. Instead of seizing the opportunities created by windows of peace to put in place long-term and predictable reconstruction commitments, aid agencies often prevaricate and channel support through humanitarian aid. There are exceptions to the rule. In countries such as Mozambique, Rwanda, Sierra Leone and the Solomon Islands, key donors moved swiftly to underpin peace settlements with financing and security guarantees (UNESCO, 2011a). Of course, supporting countries emerging from conflicts entails risks – but so does prevarication. Allowing countries to slide back into violence creates the potential for conflicts to spill across borders and destabilize regions, increasing demands on the humanitarian aid system in the process.

One of the most effective responses to risk is the pooling of aid resources. Multi-donor trust funds provide an instrument through which donors can lower transaction costs, channel resources to countries in which they have a limited bilateral presence, and deliver results. The Afghanistan Reconstruction Trust Fund (ARTF) is one example of a risk-pooling arrangement that has made a difference, not least in education. Between 2002 and 2010, around thirty-two donors channeled almost $US4 billion through the ARTF. Over the same period the share allocated to education increased from two per cent to 17%. These resources have played a critical role in supporting the construction of a national education system, in increasing enrolment, and narrowing gender gaps (OECD-DAC, 2010, Development Initiatives 2010b). One of the great weaknesses of the wider multilateral aid architecture in education is that it has provided limited support to conflict-affected states. The Fast Track initiative was singularly ineffective in this area and there are few grounds for optimism that its successor, the Global Partnership for Education, will register an improved performance (UNESCO, 2010, Dom 2009). It is in response to this failure that the former Prime Minister of the United Kingdom, Gordon Brown, has called for the creation of a new global aid facility in education with a remit that will better serve the interests of conflict-affected countries (Brown, 2011).

There are no universally applicable or clear-cut rules that can unlock the potential for education to play a greater role in peacebuilding. Just as every armed conflict is driven by different causes, so every post-conflict environment is marked by different threats and opportunities. However, with so many conflicts linked to ethnicity and belief, and fuelled by prejudice, bigotry and hostility to others, education has a pivotal role to play in changing attitudes and forging senses of identity that make societies more resilient and less vulnerable to violent conflict. Research into protracted displacement increasingly highlights the importance of these peacebuilding processes (Long, 2011). Thus education not only has a role to play in the search for peace but also, by extension, the search for a durable solution to displacement.

The starting point is to recognize that education is not a peripheral matter, but a central part of the post-conflict and peacebuilding agenda. One practical implication is that national education strategies should include an assessment of the role that the education system can play in building peace, along with an assessment of risks associated with education policies that might fuel real or perceived group-based grievances. This is another area in which aid – and aid agencies – can make a difference. Many governments in post-conflict countries lack the capacity or the financial resources to undertake post-conflict risk assessment exercises. The UN Peacebuilding Fund, which operates under the auspices of the Peacebuilding Support Office (PBSO), could provide a valuable source of institutional support. Unfortunately, it suffers from under-financing and the neglect of education (Smith, 2010).

Conclusion

The recent Global Monitoring Report has highlighted the impact that conflict continues to have on children's lives, with devastating consequences for their education. This chapter has documented the systematic failure of both national governments and the international community to ensure the educational needs of internally displaced children are fulfilled. While the primary responsibility to protect and assist IDPs lies with national authorities, children are often let down by failures in planning. Schools are used for other purposes, inflexible residency policies exclude IDPs from accessing basic services and insufficient planning for returnees result in a denial of the right to education. At other times these same authorities may be implicated in violating the rights of IDPs in the course of war. In cases such as this international humanitarian law dictates that the international community has a duty to ensure the rights of IDPs are fulfilled. Here too we have a story of systematic failure. Most of the aid directed towards conflict-affected states that are home to IDPs is channeled through the humanitarian aid system. While parents and children repeatedly demonstrate the value they place on education, the sector receives a small fraction of humanitarian aid and requests for funding are delinked from any credible needs assessment. Compared to natural disasters, conflicts are somewhat more predictable and long-term, with the average armed conflict in a low-income country lasting 12 years. An effective response to the needs of IDPs in conflict situations, especially in a sector like education, therefore requires predictable, long-term financing. However, donor caution and a binary mindset rooted in the 'humanitarian/development' divide mean that responses are characterized by short-termism. Given the links between ethnic fragmentation, inequality and conflict, these systematic failures are not only robbing displaced children of their right to education but means that we are missing important opportunities for the contribution education can play in wider peacebuilding processes and the search for a durable solution to their displacement.

Sixteen years have now passed since *Graça Machel* presented to the United Nations General Assembly her report on children trapped in armed conflict. Much has changed since then – but her report retains a powerful resonance. Reflecting on the plight of children in conflict-affected countries she wrote: 'This is a space devoid of the most basic human values…there are few further depths to which humanity can sink' (Machel, 1996). The report went on to call for decisive action on the part of the international community. As this and other chapters have demonstrated, the case for decisive action remains as compelling as ever. As governments look towards the 2015 deadline for the Millennium Development Goals, it is time to put the human rights, the hopes and the education of children caught-up in armed conflict where they belong: namely, at the center of the international development agenda.

Questions for Further Discussion

What funding mechanisms might be used to bridge the gap between humanitarian and development programming?

What implications are there for donors of a more active contribution of education to peacebuilding?

References

Bailey, S. (2009), *An Independent Evaluation of Concern Worldwide's Emergency Response in North Kivu, Democratic Republic of Congo: Responding to Displacement with Vouchers and Fairs.* London: Overseas Development Institute, Humanitarian Policy Group.

Birkenes, A. (2006), 'Justice for Colombian IDPs?' *Forced Migration Review*, 26.

Brown, G. (2011), *Education for All: Beating Poverty, Unlocking Prosperity* www.campaignforeducation. org/docs/reports/brown/EFA%20Report_Low%20Res%20v2.pdf (Accessed January 2012).

Cepeda Espinosa, M. J. (2009), 'The Constitutional Protection of IDPs in Colombia' in Rivadeneira, R. A. (ed.), *Judicial Protection of Internally Displaced Persons: The Colombian Experience.* Washington DC: Brookings-Bern Project on Internal Displacement.

Coghlan, B., Ngoy, P., Mulumba, F., Hardy, C., Bemo, V. N., Stewart, T., Lewis, J. and Brennan, R. (2008), *Mortality in the Democratic Republic of Congo: An Ongoing Crisis. New York*, International Rescue Committee, Burnet Institute.

Collier, P. (2007), *The Bottom Billion: Why the Poorest Countries Are Failing and What Can Be Done About It.* New York: Oxford University Press.

Collier, P. and Hoeffler, A. (2004), '*Greed and grievance in civil war'* in Oxford Economic Papers, 56 (4).

Development Initiatives (2010a), *GHA Report 2010.* Somerset, UK: Development Initiatives.

—(2010b), *Funding to education channelled through humanitarian and development pooled financing mechanisms in conflict-affected countries.* Background paper for EFA Global Monitoring Report 2011.

Dolan, J. and Ndaruhutse, S. (2010), *Save the Children UK's financial flows, programme choices, and the influences of the Rewrite the Future Campaign.* Background paper for EFA Global Monitoring Report 2011.

Dom, C. (2009), *FTI Mid-Term Evaluation: FTI and Fragile States and Fragile Partnerships.* Cambridge/ Oxford, UK: Cambridge Education/Mokoro/Oxford Policy Management. (Working Paper 6.).

Ferris, E. (2010a), 'Protecting the rights of internally displaced children' in Ensor, M. O. and Goêdziak, E. M. (eds), *Children and Migration. At the Crossroads of Resiliency and Vulnerability*. Basingstoke, UK: Palgrave Macmillan.

—(2010b), 'The role of municipal authorities' in *Forced Migration Review*, 34.

Ferris, E., and Winthrop, R. (2010), *Education and Displacement: Assessing Conditions for Refugees and Internally Displaced Persons affected by Conflict*. Paris: UNESCO.

Foster, M., Bennett, J., Brusset, E. and Kluyskens, J. (2010), *Country Programme Evaluation Sudan*. London, UK: Department for International Development. (Evaluation Report, EV708.)

Guha-Sapir, D. (2005), *Viewpoint: Counting Darfur's Dead Isn't Easy*. London: Reuters AlertNet. www.alertnet.org/thefacts/reliefresources/111115822420.htm (Accessed October 2010.).

IDMC (2012), 'IDP News Alert', 13th January 2012 www.internal-displacement.org/idmc/website/news.nsf/(httpIDPNewsAlerts)/A83B36440D65852EC125798400335F60?OpenDocument#anchor1 (Accessed January 2012).

IDMC (2011a), *Internal Displacement: Global Overview of Trends and Developments in 2010*. Geneva: IDMC.

—(2011b), *Afghanistan Armed Conflict Forces Increasing Numbers of Afghans to Flee their Homes*. Geneva: IDMC. www.internal-displacement.org/8025708F004BE3B1/(httpInfoFiles)/3E5B840FE3A6D72BC125786F003FF157/$file/Afghanistan+-+April+2011.pdf (Accessed January 2012).

—(2011c), *Democratic Republic of Congo*. Geneva: IDMC www.internal-displacement.org/8025708F004BE3B1/(httpInfoFiles)/111D01A00B251BE0C125790B002DFC4C/$file/DRC-Overview-Sept2011.pdf (Accessed January 2011).

—(2010), *Global Statistics*. Geneva: IDMC. www.internaldisplacement.org/8025708F004CE90B/(httpPages)/22FB1D4E2B196DAA802570BB005E787C?OpenDocument&count=1000. (Accessed January 2011).

—(2009), *Democratic Republic of Congo: Massive Displacement and Deteriorating Humanitarian Conditions*. Geneva: IDMC.

IRIN (2010), *Indepth: Congo's Refugee Crisis*. Nairobi: OCHA. www.irinnews.org/IndepthMain.aspx?InDepthID=86&ReportID=88469 (Accessed January 2012).

Lloyd, C., B., El-Kogali, S., Robinson, J. P., Rankin, J. and A. Rashed (2010), *Schooling and Conflict in Darfur: A Snapshot of Basic Education Services for Displaced Children*. New York: Population Council, Women's Refugee Council.

Machel, G. (1996), *Impact of Armed Conflict on Children*. New York: UNICEF.

Martin, E. and N. Sluga (2011), *Sanctuary in the City? HPG Working Paper*. London: ODI www.odi.org.uk/resources/docs/7492.pdf. (Accessed 20 October 2010).

Multi-Donor Trust Fund (MDTF), for Southern Sudan. (2010), *Turning the Corner: 2009 Annual Report*. New York: UNDP, Multi-Donor Trust Fund for Southern Sudan.

O'Malley, B. (2010a), *Education Under Attack 2010*. Paris: UNESCO.

—(2010b), *The Longer Term Impact of Attacks on Education on Education Systems, Development and Fragility and the Implications for Policy Responses*. Background paper for EFA Global Monitoring Report 2011.

OCHA (2010), *République Démocratique du Congo: Mouvements de Populations au 30 Septembre 2010* [Democratic Republic of the Congo: Population Movements as of 30 September 2010], United Nations Office for the Coordination of Humanitarian Affairs.

OECD (2010), *Transition Financing: Building a Better Response.* Paris: Organisation for Economic Co-operation and Development, Development Assistance Committee, International Network on Conflict and Fragility.

OECD-DAC (2010), *International Development Statistics: Creditor Reporting System.* Paris: Organisation for Economic Co-operation and Development, Development Assistance Committee. stats.oecd.org/Index.aspx?DatasetCode=CRSNEW (Accessed 16 April 2010).

Østby, G. (2008), 'Horizontal inequalities, political environment and civil conflict: evidence from 55 developing countries' in Stewart, F. (ed.), *Horizontal Inequalities and Conflict: Understanding Group Violence in Multiethnic Countries.* Basingstoke, UK: Palgrave Macmillan.

Rose, P. (2010), *Education Can't Wait Til the War is Over.* World Education Blog efareport.wordpress. com/2010/08/04/education-can%e2%80%99t-wait-till-the-war-is-over/ (Accessed January 2012).

Smith, A. (2010), 'The influence of education on conflict and peace building', Background paper prepared for the Education for All Global Monitoring Report 2011 *The Hidden Crisis: Armed conflict and education,* Paris: UNESCO.

Stewart, F. (ed.) (2008), *Horizontal Inequalities and Conflict: Understanding Group Mobilization in Multiethnic Societies.* Basingstoke, UK: Palgrave Macmillan.

United Nations (2010), *The Millennium Development Goals Report* www.un.org/millenniumgoals/ pdf/MDG%20Report%202010%20En%20r15%20-low%20res%2020100615%20-.pdf (Accessed January 2012).

UNESCO (2011a), *Education For All Global Monitoring Report 2011. The hidden crisis: Armed conflict and education.* Paris: UNESCO.

—(2011b), *Building a Better Future. Education for an Independent South Sudan.* Paris: UNESCO

—(2010), *EFA Global Monitoring Report 2010: Reaching the Marginalized.* Paris: UNESCO, Oxford University Press.

Watkins, K. (2011), *Aid Donors Get an F for Education,* Guardian Poverty Matters Blog www.guardian. co.uk/global-development/poverty-matters/2011/mar/01/unesco-report-aid-donors-education-conflict (Accessed December 2011).

World Bank (2011), *World Development Report 2011: Conflict, Security and Development.* Washington: The World Bank.

Legislative Protection for IDPs and Education in Colombia

Manuel José Cepeda Espinosa

4

Chapter Outline

Abstract

This chapter outlines the steps taken by the Colombian judicial authorities to introduce and monitor a series of instruments increasing the legislative protection of the tens of thousands of Internally Displaced Persons (IDPs) in the country following decades of internal armed conflict. The chapter examines specific legal measures undertaken with regard to securing and protecting the rights of IDPs in the national and international context, including in education, housing, land protection and health. It also highlights progress made to date in implementing the reforms alongside areas in which improvement is required as part of this extremely complex process.

Introduction[1]

As a consequence of the armed conflict that has spanned the last four decades, Colombia has one of the world's highest rates of forced internal displacement. This humanitarian crisis has placed Colombia just behind Sudan in terms of global displacement figures (IDMC, 2011). Colombia has roughly four million forcibly displaced persons within its national borders who are affected by systematic and grave violations of their fundamental rights. In 2004, paramilitary groups began a gradual demobilization process, which has so far led to the demobilization of 32,000 persons. Some paramilitaries still operate and some have rearmed themselves, but their numbers have decreased significantly in recent years. The Colombian internal armed conflict is complex and long-standing. It is currently waged in specific rural areas by three main actors: the State's armed forces, extreme-right paramilitary groups and extreme-left guerrillas.

The civilian population has borne the brunt of the violence and suffered unspeakable outrages to its most basic human rights. Colombian violence ordinarily includes acts such as massacres, selective murders, forced disappearances, extra-judicial executions, kidnappings, torture, extortion, forced recruitment of children and others by illegal armed actors, attacks against defenseless villages with internationally prohibited weapons (including, for example, rudimentary explosives such as domestic gas pipes used against civilians), blockades, confinements, mass arbitrary detentions, acts of terrorism, installation of anti-personnel mines and sexual assault of women and children. All of the parties to the conflict have been found to be responsible for such acts and victims number in the tens of thousands each year.

According to the United Nations High Commissioner for Refugees (UNHCR), the displaced population totals eight per cent of the Colombian population. However, there is disagreement over the total number of IDPs in the country. It is now commonly acknowledged that from 1995 to 2007 between three and four million Colombians were expelled from their usual places of residence or work, mainly in the countryside but also in urban settings, thereby expanding cities', towns' and villages' ever-expanding slums. Several factors also contribute significantly to the daily experience of being displaced, resulting in a complex cycle of human rights violations that degrade people's quality of life. Some of these factors are: high levels of poverty; the loss of cultural and social bonds; the abandonment of the scarce patrimonial assets held before displacement; low levels of education; the shock of having experienced traumatic acts of violence; being forced to live in alien settings with no official or social support; severe difficulties in finding employment in urban areas; limited educational opportunities for children; and limited access to social security, health and pension benefits.

Children and young peolle under 18 years of age account for over 50% of the displaced population, and their families also include significant proportions of elderly persons and individuals with disabilities, all of whom are forced to live in miserable conditions in marginal urban settlements, with the nutritional, health, educational, social and psychological consequences that inescapably arise. These consequences include: unusually high rates of premature pregnancy and child rearing; higher exposure to the risks of prostitution; forced recruitment and trafficking in human beings; initiation into criminal gangs; high levels of child and infant malnutrition; and an increase in domestic violence rates. Furthermore, the country's indigenous and Afro-Colombian populations have been disproportionately affected by forced internal displacement, and more than a dozen of the country's indigenous cultures are at high risk of extinction in the near future.

State Responses to Forced Displacement: Law 387 (1997) and Decision T-025 (2004)

State responses to the problem of forced displacement in Colombia have evolved over time. Prior to 1997 there was no specific legislation to address the issue, but the adoption by Congress of Law 387 of 1997 represented a major breakthrough. This Law, composed of 33 articles, enshrines in legal terms a distinct public policy for assisting IDPs, structured upon three main pillars. First, it includes a definition of the rights and duties of IDPs. In general terms, this is consistent with the formulation of rights and duties set forth in international instruments. Second, it creates a National Comprehensive Assistance System for the Displaced Population (SNAIPD); this includes a central coordinating council, in which Ministers and other high-level public officials have a seat. It also creates territorial councils charged with aiding in the policy's implementation at the departmental and municipal levels, and it mandates the creation of a specific national plan to address the phenomenon, as well as a national information network to facilitate the effective implementation of the system. Third, it structures the policy in accordance with three main phases of displacement: prevention and protection during displacement, emergency humanitarian aid following displacement, and socio-economic stabilization, including return and re-establishment in order to find durable solutions to displacement. Law 387 was significant in recognizing the importance of legal protection for IDPs, but initial implementation was poor and led to hundreds of *tutela* petitions by IDPs during 2003.

In 2004, after reviewing over one hundred *tutela* files, the Colombian Constitutional Court formally declared that the fundamental rights of the country's internally displaced persons were being disregarded in such a massive, protracted and reiterated manner, that an 'unconstitutional state of affairs' had arisen (Colombian Constitutional Court 2004)[2]. This conclusion was reached after verifying that the competent authorities were not addressing the extremely vulnerable conditions of IDPs. This conclusion was also reached because the Court found that responsibility rested not only with the actions or omissions of a single State entity, but also as a consequence of structural factors affecting the entire public policy for assisting the displaced population. The result, the Court concluded, caused a wide gap between the formal, legal definition of the policy's components (as reflected in Law 387 of 1997) and the financial resources allocated for the policy's execution (as well as the State's inadequate institutional capacity to implement the policy). The Court therefore identified two main factors that accounted for the State's incapacity to respond adequately to the needs of the displaced population to protect its rights effectively: (i) the precariousness of the institutional capacity to implement the policy, and (ii) the insufficient appropriation of funds.

As a consequence of the State's inability to afford IDPs timely and effective protection, the Court held that their rights to personal integrity, equality, petition, work, health, social security, education, minimum subsistence income, housing, land protection, return and re-establishment and to a dignified life were all being continually violated on account of the unconstitutional state of affairs. It also declared that special protection of elderly persons, women (especially female heads of households), children and members of ethnic groups – all of which comprise a significant proportion of the country's displaced population – was not being provided.

The formal declaration of an unconstitutional state of affairs enabled the Court to adopt a decision for the benefit of the entire displaced population in the country, and not just for the specific plaintiffs in the *tutela* cases under review. Prior to this judgment, the Court had declared an unconstitutional state of affairs on nine different occasions, in which the following factual elements were present: a repeated and constant violation of fundamental rights, affecting a multitude of persons, due to problems of a structural nature and requiring the intervention of several State authorities for its resolution. As was the case in Decision T-025 of 2004, the Court issued complex orders to protect the rights, not only of the plaintiffs who filed *tutela* lawsuits, but also of *all* the persons who shared the same situation and who had not resorted to judicial channels. These orders included the design and implementation of the relevant policies, plans and programs, the appropriation of the necessary funds in national and territorial budgets, the modification of administrative practices, the resolution of organizational and procedural flaws, the amendment of the relevant legal framework, or the advancement of administrative, budgetary or contracting procedures required to guarantee the fundamental rights at risk. In Decision T-025 of 2004, the Court followed this doctrine and adopted the corresponding remedies, ordering the national and territorial authorities to adopt the required corrective measures within their own spheres of competency. However, the unconstitutional state of affairs declared in this decision implied a significant advance in the scope and effects of such doctrine.

One novel aspect of the declaration of an unconstitutional state of affairs in the field of internal displacement is that after its adoption the Court retained its jurisdiction over the case and issued a series of follow-up awards (*Autos*). In these awards, the Court verified the level of compliance given to its orders over time, fine-tuned some of the details, and issued specific instructions to the authorities aimed at securing the adoption of the measures required to advance in an accelerated and sustained manner towards the resolution of the identified problems. Moreover, these awards have required the entities that form part of the SNAIPD to submit periodical reports to the Court, describing the manner in which they have fulfilled the mandates issued therein – a feature which had not been present before.

Second, a number of awards were issued to supervise the constitutionality of the general public policy for assisting the displaced population, and to oversee the resolution of the unconstitutional state of affairs declared in Decision T-025 of 2004. Several awards have been issued in this field, dealing with different aspects of the policy. One should highlight those that deal with the adoption of a rational set of public policy indicators based on the criterion of 'effective enjoyment of rights', and those that strive to bridge the gap between the national and the territorial authorities, fostering their coordination so as better to overcome the existing situation. The latest group of decisions along this line was adopted in early 2009, after analyzing the policy in the light of the criterion of 'effective enjoyment of fundamental rights'.

Third, a number of awards have been issued to address highly specific situations, or aspects of the public policy, that warrant the Court's intervention because there exists at least one of the following scenarios: a risk to a specific displaced population, a visible gap in the public policy, or a risk derived from the armed conflict that may cause massive displacement in the foreseeable future. For example, the Court ordered the Government, in Award 248 of 2008, to address the serious and urgent problem caused to both displaced and non-displaced populations by anti-personnel mines in the southern municipality of Samaniego.

Principles Underlying the Court's Decisions in the Field of Forced Internal Displacement

In designing and adopting Decision T-025 of 2004 and its follow-up awards, the Court took a number of steps to preserve a balance between its role as an arbiter of human rights and its deference for the executive and legislative powers. The main principles can be summarized as follows:

- **Constitutional rights were directly incorporated into the public policy for the protection of the displaced population.** The immediate impact of this incorporation was to cause a reformulation and re-visualization of the policy, which is now oriented towards the effective enjoyment of constitutional rights, and includes a component of judicial control.
- **Balancing of rights and establishing minimum, mandatory levels of satisfaction under any circumstance.** The Court applied a balancing method to incorporate the complexities of the factual situation in which the rights of IDPs were being disregarded. In this way, it analyzed the conditions of vulnerability in which the plaintiffs and other IDPs were living in the light of the State's financial constraints and the existing institutional capabilities to attend to the requirements of this massive segment of the population. As a result of having weighed the diverse factors, the Court crafted a creative set of remedies that exacted minimum degrees of satisfaction of the affected constitutional rights and the design and implementation of a rational public policy to assist them. It did so while also paying due attention to the State's institutional limitations and realistic possibilities

of overcoming the crisis. The Court concluded that the minimum rights of IDPs include the following: the right to life; the rights to dignity and to physical, psychological and moral integrity; the right to family life and to family unity and reunification; the right to a basic level of subsistence, including food, water, shelter, clothing, essential medical services and sanitation, obtained chiefly through the provision of emergency humanitarian aid; the right to health care, particularly in cases of children and infants; the right to protection from discrimination based on the conditions of IDPs; the right to basic education for children under 15; the right to self-sufficiency through the identification of alternatives for dignified socioeconomic stabilization; and the rights to return and re-establishment. The Court also asserted that authorities have obligations to secure a minimum level of satisfaction of these rights through positive actions.

- **Respect for other authorities' spheres of jurisdiction.** As a consequence of the Court's awareness of the complexity of the situation, that required coordinated action by several different State entities, the orders issued in the judgment respected the different spheres of jurisdiction of the executive branch, Congress and other competent authorities.

- **Requirement of gradual satisfaction of the affected rights.** The Court's approach has been marked by gradualism. It has not ordered a full resolution of the problem, not even within a specific period of time. The Court has, however, ordered the competent authorities to pursue an accelerated, sustained solution to the unconstitutional state of affairs through the adoption of any measures they deem necessary for the achievement of that purpose. That is why the issue of the *result indicators* has become so important. Should the Court remain focused, within its gradual approach, on the mere adoption of measures aimed at overcoming the problems, without requiring accelerated advances towards the effective enjoyment of rights, the competent authorities would always be able to say that they have carried out more meetings, appropriated more funds and assigned more public officials to the relevant task. But this would be a gradual approach centred merely on process, rather than on the material effects of the process of achieving the enjoyment of the rights in question. That is why in the 2005 follow-up decisions the Court decided to fine-tune its gradual approach, shifting its focus towards the results of the public policy's implementation. It has accelerated and sustained advances, measurable on the basis of clear indicators, of the policy goals set by the competent authorities themselves. In the end the policy goals must achieve the effective enjoyment of rights by a large proportion of displaced persons.

- **Focus on the effective enjoyment of constitutional rights.** More than ordering mere respect for IDPs' rights, the Court has also centered its attention on their effective enjoyment and has required certain actions to be carried out in accordance with its results-centered gradual approach. For instance, this has required the executive branch to undertake affirmative measures aimed at providing protection to IDPs. This protection has two levels. First, specific actions are aimed at the provision of aid, the opening of opportunities, the facilitation of access. Second, programs and strategies are designed from a medium term perspective, for the purpose of improving the institutional infrastructure for the protection of IDPs. However, the Court has understood that the design and implementation of indicators based on the effective enjoyment of constitutional rights is a complex task with technical components. For this reason, it initiated a process of information exchange that culminated in Award 109 of 2007, in which the Court ordered the Government to adopt a set of effective rights-enjoyment indicators to measure the advances of the policy on the ground. For example, the Government is not only to report on efforts to obtain additional resources, but also on how the actual increase in public expenditure has improved the access of IDPs to humanitarian aid, food, housing, health services and education.

- **Preserving minimum levels of protection for IDPs' rights.** Within the aforementioned gradual approach, which is targeted towards the effective enjoyment of constitutional rights, a specific problem has arisen for the Court, namely that of preventing the transformation of basic rights into "progressive development rights" (i.e. how to avoid a situation in which the Court admits a gradual satisfaction of rights, such as to life or integrity, which should on principle be secured in an immediate and effective manner). In order to overcome this risk, the Court demanded the satisfaction of certain minimum levels of enjoyment of IDPs' fundamental rights. That is to say, Decision T-025 of 2004 and its follow-up awards adopted an approach based on gradualism, but on the grounds of having secured a minimum degree of satisfaction of certain essential rights, which are *not* subject to progressive development.

Mobilization of the State and Society Around the Protection of IDPs

The Court has sought to mobilize the State and society around the protection of IDPs. Some manifestations of this approach are as follows:

(i) Since the adoption of the judgment, the Court has required that decisions adopted by CNAIPD include the participation of displaced persons and their organizations. This has had the effect of mobilizing and empowering IDPs, and helps focus their activities on public policies that benefit them.

(ii) State entities have also been mobilized, in the sense that the Court has issued orders which imply an exercise of mutual comparison between them, so as to establish which is advancing the most, which is producing the best results and which is lagging behind the rest. This reciprocal comparison increased the visibility of their respective actions and omissions, and has catalyzed authorities' efforts to resolve IDPs' problems.

(iii) The issue of coordination has been granted increasing importance, both at the national level and in regard to the territorial entities. In one of its follow-up decisions, the Court identified the overall coordination of SNAIPD and the coordination of territorial entities' efforts as two of the critical areas where significant gaps existed in the policy's implementation, and where the most important improvements were required.

(iv) Different State oversight authorities have also been mobilized, not by means of Court orders, but through requests issued in Decision T- 025 of 2004 and its follow-up decisions. Therefore, the disciplinary and budgetary oversight authorities, the Controller's Office and the Public Prosecutor's Office, and the Public Ombudsman's office (*Defensoría del Pueblo*), which have available infrastructure and staff across the national territory, have incorporated the issue of internal displacement into their agendas. Additionally, they have provided critical follow-up support and have submitted the relevant information to the Court.

(v) Congress has also been mobilized around internal displacement. Although the results are less visible, a number of congressional debates on the issue have already taken place. The Court has requested the inclusion of the issue of displacement in the national budget and the national development plan (both of which are approved by Congress), which entails the advancement of democratic debate on the level of priority afforded to the topic, and on public policy as such.

(iv) Civil society has been mobilized around the issue of forced internal displacement. The most significant development in this area is the creation of the Civil Society Follow-up Commission on the Public Policy on Internal Displacement, created as a forum that gathers representatives of IDP organizations, NGOs, indigenous peoples, Afro-Colombian groups and academia, with the task of closely overseeing the actions and programs adopted by the different competent authorities for the resolution of the unconstitutional state of affairs and compliance with the Court's orders.

In short, through the mobilization of different authorities and of civil society, the Court has managed not only to include the problem of displacement in the national agenda, but to keep it there and maintain its visibility. This is all the more significant considering that the Colombian public agenda is quite crowded, and the issues included therein tend to become invisible over time (especially if they concern traditionally weak segments of the population that lack strong voices, as in the case of displaced persons). In adopting follow-up decisions by mobilizing State entities and by receiving and analyzing periodic reports, the Court has managed to keep the plight of displaced persons visible.

Implications for the Education of IDPs

Regarding the design and regulatory development of the policy, the Court identified seven salient problems: (i) the lack of a plan of action for the overall national system of assistance, precluding it from having a global view of the policy and its operation; (ii) a lack of specific goals, priorities or indicators; (iii) a vague distribution of functions and responsibilities between the different participating state entities; (iv) a perceived absence of policy elements regarded as fundamental by its implementing agencies; (v) a lack of implementation and development of many of the policy's elements, including those recognition of gender-, ethnicity- and age-based specificities among the target population; (vi) the excessive rigidity of the system's design in the provision of emergency humanitarian aid; and (vii) a lack of clarity in the distribution of functions among competent entities in the field of urban productive projects. The Court also noted that in certain cases the means used to achieve policy aims were not appropriate, for example:

> 'As to education, requiring displaced households to pay a minimum payable amount so that displaced persons of schooling age can gain access to educational positions has been an – often insurmountable – barrier for these minors' registration in the system' (Colombian Constitutional Court 2004: 6.1.3.2.)

The decision of the Court concerned the realization of a broad set of rights for IDPs, but the decision highlighted the right to basic education for children under 15 (article 67, paragraph 3, of the Constitution). The Chamber clarified that 'even though Principle 23 establishes the State duty to provide basic primary education to the displaced population, the scope of the international obligation described therein is broadened by article 67 of the Constitution, by virtue of which education shall be mandatory between five and fifteen years of age, and it must comprise at least one pre-school year and nine years of basic education. The State is bound, at the minimum to secure the provision of a school seat for each displaced child within the age of mandatory education, in a public educational institution. That is to say, the State's minimum duty in regards to the education of displaced children is to secure their access to education, through the provision of the seats that are necessary in public or private entities of the area'. This was the order issued by the Court in Decision T-215 of 2002 to the respondent Municipal Education Secretariat: to secure access to the educational system by the plaintiff children, using the available places in the schools of the area. This preferential treatment for displaced children is justified, not only because education is one of their fundamental rights, as happens with all the other children in the national territory, but because of their especially vulnerable conditions they receive reinforced constitutional protection. In the field of education this means that if at least their basic education is not secured, the effects of displacement upon their personal autonomy and the exercise of their rights will be worsened.

Contributions of the Judgment and its Follow-up Decisions

Decision T-025 of 2004 and its follow-up awards have not only contributed significantly to the effective protection of IDPs' rights, but also to the development of complex legal notions and current constitutional debates which will be instrumental for future actions. These contributions in the Colombian context are explained below.

Indivisibility of rights

The Court adopted a comprehensive approach towards the rights of IDPs, conceptualizing these rights as an indivisible group that includes first-generation rights (life, integrity, equality, basic freedoms), economic, social and cultural rights (health, education, housing, minimum subsistence income) and even collective rights (such as those of ethnic groups). This indivisibility was expressed in three main ways:

(i) From a procedural standpoint, all the rights were protected simultaneously – the Court refrained from adopting a judgment exclusively in relation to the affected *fundamental* rights, and it did not resort to its prior doctrine of 'connection' (*conexidad*) between fundamental and non-fundamental constitutional rights. Instead, it granted protection to the entire set of rights enjoyed by IDPs, rights which were understood to be inseparable from one another.

(ii) The Court also defined minimum levels of satisfaction for several different rights, which had to be simultaneously secured, and that were ultimately grounded in the need to secure a dignified life within the parameters of respect for the diversity and specificity of each affected person.

(iii) In addition, the Court emphasized that all the rights that form part of this indivisible group have both a negative and a positive dimension. In other words, they impose both positive and negative duties and obligations upon the State.

> Thus, from the traditional viewpoint (where first-generation rights only impose negative duties of respect and non-violation upon States, and where second-generation rights impose positive duties of satisfaction), the Court held that all types of rights generate both types of obligations for authorities and society alike. This implies, moreover, that in the Court's view, all the protected rights have a specific economic cost that must be assumed by the State, given that there are no rights with a merely negative dimension.

Incorporation of public international law into the rationale of the judgment

In order to justify its decision in legal terms, the Court relied on two main sources of authority:

(i) its own prior case-law, in which it upheld not only the rights of displaced persons but also social, economic and cultural rights, as well as collective rights; and (ii) the applicable rules of public international law, namely those found in the Guiding Principles on Internal Displacement compiled by the Representative of the UN Secretary-General for Internal Displacement in 1998. These principles specify the relevant treaty-based and customary rules in the fields of human rights law, international humanitarian law and, by analogy, international refugee law. The principles were applied by the Court as basic criteria to determine the scope of IDPs' fundamental rights and the extent of the State's obligations to protect them.

Development and application of a complex notion of 'progressiveness'

Several aspects of the Court's judgment and its follow-up decisions have emphasized the notion of 'progressiveness' in the protection and materialization of constitutional rights. Even though it has usually been accepted that certain types of rights – mostly rights of an economic, social or cultural nature – are subject to progressive development on account of the types of obligations they impose upon States, the Court explored the relationship between a progressive development of rights and the protection of an essential nucleus or minimum level of protection that must always be afforded under any circumstance. Indeed, the Court applied this 'minimum level of protection' doctrine in relation to the entire displaced population and the entire set of constitutional rights, regardless of whether they were first-, second- or third-generation rights.

A second noteworthy aspect of the way the Court dealt with progressiveness in its decisions is that it recognized the progressive development of IDPs' rights with regard to the coverage of the assistance policy (that is, the number of IDPs who receive protection) to the quality of the policy itself, and to the construction of the State's institutional capacity to protect IDPs. Thus the Court has not required emergency humanitarian aid to be provided to the entire displaced population at once, but rather has ordered the achievement of steady progress towards that goal. Likewise, the Court has not required the provision of top-quality emergency humanitarian aid, but it has established a minimum baseline for its provision. For instance, at the most basic level, displaced women or displaced families with children should be provided a humanitarian aid kit that satisfies their specific needs.

Regarding the construction of institutional capacity, the Court has ordered CNAIPD to design its own plan for overcoming the existing flaws, and it has allowed authorities reasonable periods of time to strengthen their capacity to provide assistance. For example, reforms initiated by *Acción Social* have fostered cooperation agreements with entities like the Red Cross or NGOs in order to provide timely aid to IDPs. The budgetary aspects of the policy can also be gradually developed over time. Thus, according to the goals and estimates set by the Government, the Court has accepted that the amount of resources included in the national budget is to be progressively increased over the course of several years. Indeed, the Court has not ordered the budgetary authorities to appropriate a specific amount of money to finance the policy, but rather ordered them to establish their own timetables and programs, so as to secure the gradual satisfaction of the diverse needs of IDPs.

Governmental accountability to judicial authorities

One salient effect of Decision T-025 of 2004 and its follow-up decisions has been to bind the Government to submit periodic reports to the Court, informing it about the results of the policy's implementation and the resolution of the different problems that the Court has identified. It is not only noteworthy that the Court issued this order, but also that the Government has abided by it (with the exception of some areas where the Court has had to invoke contempt of Court powers against specific mid-level public officials). This has established a dynamic of inter-institutional dialogue among the different branches of government. This dialogue provides a solid guarantee that the results of the assistance policy will improve over time.

Extension of the effects of the judgment

On account of the declaration of an unconstitutional state of affairs, the effects of Decision T-025 of 2004 and its follow-up decisions have been extended beyond the plaintiffs, in order to cover an entire segment of the population that is in constant evolution. Thus persons who became displaced after January 2004 are also covered by the orders issued therein. These orders relate to an unknown, but measurable and determinable universe of people (i.e. to the 'forcibly displaced population' in the country) and can therefore provide newly-displaced persons with the full range of benefits awarded to the specific plaintiffs and to the pre-existing IDPs. Thus in August 2007, for example, the Court adopted Award 200, which protected the right to personal security of IDP leaders who were not plaintiffs in the original *tutela* cases of 2003. Moreover, in 2007 the Court convened public hearings dedicated to the evaluation of governmental actions concerning vulnerable IDP groups. The first concerned women, the second children, the third indigenous peoples, the fourth Afro-Colombians, and, in the future, additional hearings will address the situation of the elderly and disabled. In these hearings, IDPs who were not plaintiffs in the original 2003 *tutelas* could participate.

The Implementation in the New Institutional Context

The implementation and follow up of T-025 continued after two significant changes in the institutional context, mainly the renovation of the Court and the inauguration of a new government. In 2009, seven new justices arrived at the Court. To underline the significance of T-025, the Plenary of the Court assumed the follow-up and created a special three justices Chamber to do it and report to the Plenary. In August 2010, with the inauguration of a new President came a different government which politically endorsed the need for the protection of the victims of the armed conflict.

The special Chamber of the Court complemented the follow-up in four main aspects: a call on some territorial authorities to report directly to the Court about the protection of IDPs in their jurisdictions, a specific concern for the situation of Afro–Colombian communities of the Pacific coast, a call on the National Public Prosecutor, the *Procuraduría*, and the Comptroller General to report on sanctions imposed against violators of IDP's rights and negligent officials, and an evaluation of the initiatives of the incoming government. In this last aspect, the Court issued in 2011 a follow-up order in which the Court did a very detailed study of 14 specific areas of public policy regarding IDPs. One of the areas considered was the right to education.

The Court concluded that the 'state of unconstitutional affairs' remains, even though it recognized advances in several areas. Regarding the right to education, the Court affirmed that although the data submitted by the Government indicated a progression (approximately 86% of IDPs between 5 and 17 years old attend a formal educational institution), certain inconsistencies in the figures and concern for the quality of education conditions prevented the Court from asserting that there had been complete compliance with the orders issued in Decision T-025. Consequently the Court required the Minister of Education to submit promptly a consolidated report containing figures in terms of result indicators that show the advance in the effective enjoyment of the right to education. Should the Court conclude from this new report that the actions undertaken by the Government demonstrate sufficient advance in the protection of education rights, the Court would adopt a less stringent monitoring system, as was done with respect to the right to health.

On the other hand, the new government took unprecedented actions to protect the rights of victims of the armed conflict. It adopted and implanted an ambitious program of land restitution. In June 2011, Congress enacted the Victims' Rights and Land Restitution Law, introduced by the executive, seeking to compensate victims of breaches to international humanitarian law and human rights violations. It provided measures concerning each component of reparation: restitution, compensation, satisfaction, rehabilitation and guarantees of non-repetition. Although the new law is not exclusively directed towards victims of forced displacement, it incorporates many of the orders issued by the Constitutional Court in Decision T-025 and its follow-up awards. First, it comprises a list of guiding principles mirroring those established by the Court. Among them, the law includes the principle of 'differential approach' towards the needs of differentiated groups of victims, especially women and children, for whom special provisions were established. Secondly, the law includes a list of victims' rights iterated in international standards. Thirdly, it establishes a mixed judicial/administrative system that allows IDPs whose land has been illegally seized as a result of forced displacement, to claim expeditiously for its restitution. For this purpose, the law grants some advantages derived from the relaxation of evidentiary burdens and presumptions of spoil. Finally, the law establishes a system of participation allowing victims to take part in the design, implementation, and evaluation of policy at the national, departmental, municipal and district levels.

The Law 1448 of 2011 represents a major step in the recognition of victims' rights and a comprehensive attempt towards their reparation. However, some limitations may be pointed out. First, free access to education and healthcare is subject to the victims' budgetary capacity, thus limiting the principle of gratuity. Second, result indicators in the effective enjoyment of the constitutional rights of IDPs developed by the Court in Decision T-025 and its follow-up awards receive little attention. Finally, the law grants broad discretion to the administrative authorities responsible for IDPs. Therefore the success and effectiveness of the measures contemplated by the law rely largely on further regulation adopted by state agencies. The constitutionality of many articles has been challenged before the Constitutional Court.

Conclusion

It can be argued that in the case of Colombia, the right to education for children of IDPs has been strengthened by the Court's decisions on internal displacement. Some of the most important achievements can be summarized as securing increases and rationalization of the budget for IDPs; improvement of public institutional capacities for the provision of quality assistance; some rationalization, organization and expansion of the public policy for the assistance of displaced persons; formal incorporation of the public policy into legal instruments; thorough involvement of authorities at every level of government; higher transparency and accountability in policy design and execution. Throughout, the approach has been to regard the right to education as a fundamental and integral part of a broader set of rights for IDPs.

Even though important achievements and advances have been made thus far, there are still very important aspects of the assistance policy where improvements are yet to be made, or where significant delays have been identified. First, due to the general complexity of the problem of displacement, the Court, in requiring a basic rationality in the progressive development of the public policy, has had to tolerate the continuation of certain impingements upon the constitutional rights of IDPs. The Court has had to adopt a realistic point of view, in the sense that it cannot order the final resolution of such a serious crisis, but it can – and indeed has – ordered an end to the unconstitutional state of affairs. Secondly, it appears that the State has been unable to implement the reforms required to strengthen its institutional capacity. Even though some restructuring efforts have taken place in priority areas, and although there has been a general climate of demanding results from the authorities, the State's capacity to reform itself has been overwhelmed by the magnitude of the problems to be solved. Thirdly, on account of the lack of specificity of the policy to assist the displaced, IDPs are placed in a position where they have to compete with other vulnerable and poor segments of the population for limited resources. Since Decision T-025 of 2004, the Court warned that special needs of IDPs should be addressed in the design and implementation of relevant programs. However, although important progress has been made, this result is yet to be attained in some crucial areas, such as education and housing. Fourthly, the Charter of Basic Rights of Displaced Persons, which provides a summary of IDPs' rights enumerated by the Court in Decision T-025 of 2004, has not had the impact that it should have had. Most IDPs are still unaware of the extent of their constitutional rights. Nevertheless, while significantly stronger efforts are needed, some advances have been made in the dissemination of the Charter through the activities of leaders and civil society organizations. Fifthly, even though the displaced population has been substantially empowered to assume the defence of its own rights, the degree of its participation in the decision-making processes that concern it is still very low. IDP participation is dispersed, and it tends to focus on short-term demands. Nonetheless, the work of the National Follow-up Commission has in part compensated for this problem. Moreover, since the Court started issuing awards to protect IDPs with specific needs, their participation has become more effective and coordinated. However, there is still a long way to go. Lastly, the authorities' obligation to provide periodic reports to the Constitutional Court on the results of the policy entails a very clear risk of formalism, as their efforts may focus on the mere elaboration of the reports, rather than the activities required to ensure the effective enjoyment of the constitutional rights of IDPs.

Education provision for IDP children represents a core area within a broader set of IDP rights that may be afforded legal protection. However, the permanent migration of the newly displaced population into most of the country's municipalities has provided a significant reminder of the law's inherent limitations in the face of a complex and protracted armed conflict. Regardless of how strongly IDPs' constitutional rights are protected by the country's judges, the persistence (and, in some instances, the intensification) of the conflict in Colombia will continue to generate masses of uprooted citizens who flee to the cities and towns seeking protection. The right to education of IDP children may be advanced to a degree by a judicial decision, but that will only be part of the solution and the situation may only be further improved through a peace agreement that that can provide lasting solutions to the causes of the underlying humanitarian crisis.

Questions for Further Discussion

To what extent can rights be fully protected at a judicial level in the absence of complete political stability?

How can international law play a proactive role in bolstering and reinforcing rights protecting initiatives within states?

Notes

1 The information included in this description of the problem of forced internal displacement in Colombia has been taken from the different reports and assessments submitted to the Constitutional Court by governmental, non-governmental and international sources. Specific figures and detailed assessments may be found on the corresponding websites: www.accion-social.gov.co (for the official governmental data), www.codhes.org (for the information produced by the different organizations of the displaced population and the Church), or www.acnur.org (for the different reports produced and compiled by the office of the UN High Commissioner for Refugees).

2 Colombian Constitutional Court, Decision T-025 of 2004, adopted by the third chamber of the Court, composed by Manuel José Cepeda-Espinosa, Jaime Córdoba-Triviño and Rodrigo Escobar-Gil.

References

IDMC (2011), *Internal Displacement: Global Overview of Trends and Developments in 2010*. Geneva: IDMC.

Colombian Constitutional Court (2004), *Third Review Chamber, Decision T-025* Unofficial translation commissioned by Brookings-Bern can be found online www.brookings.edu/~/media/Files/rc/papers/2009/11_judicial_protection_arango/11_judicial_protection_arango.pdf (Accessed 10 December 2011).

Educational Challenges of Conflict and Flood-related Displacement in Pakistan

5

Elizabeth Ferris and Chareen Stark

Chapter Outline

Abstract

The chapter examines the consequences of conflict and flooding in Pakistan on the access to education by internally displaced persons (IDPs). The chapter begins with a short overview of internal displacement in Pakistan, both conflict and flood-related, and of education in Pakistan. It then examines the effects of the conflict and floods on education, including in terms of access by internally displaced children and host communities to education, including in camps and host communities for the conflict-affected; issues of teacher availability; primary versus secondary enrollment; the use of schools as temporary shelters for IDPs; damage to schools; and international and government efforts to provide education for IDPs affected by conflict and floods.

Introduction

Internal displacement in most countries is a complex phenomenon, but is particularly so in the case of Pakistan due to the combination of long-standing civil-military conflict, a devastating earthquake, periodic counterinsurgency campaigns, and two successive years of widespread flooding in 2010 and 2011, all of which have displaced people. Displacement is a dynamic phenomenon: in some cases, individuals have returned to their communities even as both new and secondary displacements occur. During displacement, some IDPs live in government-administered camps or temporary shelters such as schools, but most live with host families or dispersed in communities where they are less visible to international humanitarian actors. Definitive estimates of the numbers of displaced persons are therefore difficult to obtain, particularly when a majority of IDPs live among host communities and may not want to be identified as IDPs.

As other chapters in this volume have indicated, displacement causes difficulties for education: schools are damaged or destroyed, teachers are displaced, government systems of support are disrupted. Even when schools are available, children may not be able to access them because they have lost the documentation necessary to enroll in schools or because continued insecurity leads parents to keep children home or because economic necessity leads displaced children to drop out of school to help support the family. When displacement becomes protracted – and particularly when children stay out of school for years – it becomes more difficult for them to resume their education. Principle 23 of the Guiding Principles on Internal Displacement affirms that 'everyone has a right to education' and that 'education and training facilities shall be made available to all internally displaced persons… whether or not they are living in camps […]' (UN Commission on Human Rights, 1998), and yet, as will be seen below, it has been particularly difficult for IDP children to access education.

Conflict, Floods and Education in Pakistan: A Brief Overview

There has been recurrent conflict between militant groups and Pakistan's armed forces since 2004 which has caused considerable internal displacement. Army operations in South Waziristan from 2004–6 reportedly displaced tens of thousands of people and clashes in Balochistan from 2005–7 displaced tens of thousands more. Government operations against militants in South Waziristan and then against Taliban insurgents in the Swat Valley in 2007 led to further displacement. While many reportedly returned in 2008, renewed government operations in North West Frontier Province (NWFP) led to the displacement of at least two million people in the span of a few weeks. This marked the largest population movement in Pakistan since Partition in 1947, and by the end of 2009, the country had the sixth largest conflict-induced IDP population in the world (IDMC, 2010a).

Overall, conflict between Pakistan's armed forces and militant groups led to the internal displacement of an estimated 3.3 million people in northwest Pakistan between 2008 and 2010. Approximately two million of those internally displaced were children, 85–90% of whom lived in host communities, in accordance with Pashtun tradition (IDMC, 2010b; UN Children's Fund (UNICEF), 2009).[1] Access to education was among the problems internally displaced children faced, despite efforts by the government of Pakistan, UN agencies, international humanitarian organizations, NGOs and communities themselves (IDMC, 2010b). In response to the 2005 earthquake, the international community had implemented a cluster system, including an Education Cluster, to coordinate humanitarian response. The cluster was also operational during the conflict-induced displacement crisis of 2008–10 and was reactivated in the 2010 floods.

With the government promoting rapid returns of IDP families beginning in July 2009 – contrary to the principles of voluntary, safe and dignified return – an estimated two-thirds of internally displaced children had returned to their home areas by mid-2010 (IDMC, 2010b). However, factors including the lack of funding for the Education Cluster and the slow pace of rebuilding and rehabilitating damaged schools, as well as security concerns, meant that children in return areas lacked access to working schools (IDMC, 2010b).

While displacement in the northwest received considerable attention, there are other patterns of displacement in Pakistan – particularly in Balochistan – which are less well known. Balochistan is geographically a huge territory, its population is relatively small and it remains disadvantaged in comparison to the rest of the country. According to 2007 reports, Balochistan has the lowest literacy rate countrywide, the fewest educational institutions, the lowest ranking on gender parity and is generally considered the poorest region in the country with the highest infant mortality (International Crisis Group, 2007: 9). Since independence in 1947, there have been various wars due to insurgencies and in December 2005 the army's 35,000 paramilitary troops stationed in Balochistan launched full-scale operations against the Baloch insurgents, with 84,000 displaced by the end of 2006 according to UN estimates (IDMC, 2009: 68). International access to Balochistan has been extremely limited as a result of both government restrictions and insecurity.

Against this backdrop of ongoing conflict in Balochistan and intense counterinsurgency campaigns in the northwest, in mid-2010 Pakistan was struck by intense and prolonged monsoon rains which were unprecedented in the country's history. The heavy rainfall and resulting floods of the Indus River Basin, which flows north to south, created a moving body of water the size of the United Kingdom. The floods marked the largest disaster ever recorded globally in terms of the area impacted, people affected and homes damaged. Further, in total, a wider area and more people have been affected by these floods than those affected by the Indian Ocean Tsunami, Hurricane Katrina, the 2005 South Asia earthquake and the Haiti 2010 earthquake combined (Polastro et al., 2011). The floods swept through the four regions of Khyber Pakhtunkhwa, Sindh, Punjab and Balochistan, affecting over 20 million people – over one-tenth of the population – in 84 of Pakistan's 121 districts. Nearly 2,000 people lost their lives and millions were homeless and displaced; more than 12 million people required humanitarian assistance (UNHCR/Protection Cluster Working Group, 2011; United States Agency for International Development, 2010). An estimated 2.9 million households were affected, 1.9 million of which were severely affected or completely destroyed. The $9.7 billion in damages was almost double the damages due to the 2005 earthquake, affecting infrastructure, crops, agricultural land, livestock, homes, as well as other direct and indirect losses. An estimated 80% of food reserves were lost, driving up food prices while purchasing power fell. (Asian Development Bank and World Bank, 2010a; Polastro et al., 2011).

Education was among the sectors particularly impacted, with schools washed away, damaged or destroyed. The schooling of up to 1.3 million children was disrupted in all provinces, with damage and destruction of over 10,000 schools totaling over $310 million in direct damages. These schools accounted for 6.2% of the total institutions in Pakistan and 12% of the total institutions in the affected districts. The two worst-affected provinces were Sindh and Punjab, where respectively 18.5% and 8.8% of the pre-flood educational facilities were damaged or destroyed, followed by 12.9% and 5.6% of pre-flood facilities damaged in Balochistan and Khyber Pakhtunkhwa (Asian Development Bank and World Bank, 2010b; UN General Assembly, 2011).

The country was still recovering from the 2010 floods when once again, beginning in August 2011, major floods affected 5.4 million people and the government and international community mobilized to provide assistance. The impact of the 2011 floods was concentrated in one of the worst-hit provinces in 2010, Sindh, but also affected parts of Balochistan and Kohistan district in the north-west.

In order to place the impact of the conflict and floods on the access and quality of education for internally displaced children and youth in a broader context, this chapter turns to a brief overview of the state of education in Pakistan before the floods.

Education in Pakistan: A Snapshot

Pakistan has a weak track record in the realm of education, reflected in the fact that it ranks near the bottom on education indicators among South Asian countries. Only two per cent of Pakistan's gross domestic product was allocated to education before the 2010 floods – the lowest level in South Asia – and over 20% of children across the country were not enrolled in school (Oxfam, 2011; South Asian Forum for Education Development, 2011). In fact, one in ten of the world's out-of-school children is Pakistani and it seems highly unlikely that Pakistan will reach the Millennium Development educational goal by 2015 (Pakistan Education Task Force, 2011). Most of Pakistan's enrolled children attend government schools, but private school enrollment has increased since 1990, particularly in rural areas where they are increasingly prevalent (Das, and Andrabi, 2010; Winthrop, and Graff, 2010). In comparison to government schools, private schools have been found to be of better quality on average, including in terms of student-teacher ratio (Andrabi, et al., 2002).

Adult literacy is very low in Pakistan, with higher rates in urban areas and among men. The literacy rate for 2008–9 stood at 57% according to the government of Pakistan (Federal Bureau of Statistics, 2010). In 2009, literacy rates among girls over 14 in North West Frontier Province (NWFP, officially renamed to Khyber Pakhtunkhwa province in 2010) stood at 22% while in Federally Administered Tribal Areas (FATA), only seven per cent of girls over ten were literate (UNICEF, 2009). While overall female literacy rates have risen over time, there has been uneven progress across the provinces. Gender disparity is evident in primary gross educational enrollment rates, which were reported to be 74% for boys, compared to only 57% for girls (IDMC, 2010b).

Among the flood-affected population, a protection assessment on the Watan aid scheme conducted by the Protection Cluster Working Group revealed that the literacy rate 'appears to be even lower than the national average, with only three per cent of the respondents reporting themselves to be educated' (UN High Commissioner for Refugees (UNHCR)/Protection Cluster Working Group, 2011: 20).

Pakistan's poor performance on education indicators has been the subject of intense internal debate and has led to the creation of the Pakistan Education Task Force and the declaration by the Prime Minister that 2011 is the 'year of education.' The task force, spearheaded by the Ministry of Education, mandated by the Prime Minister of Pakistan and supported by the government of the United Kingdom, recognizes previous education policy failures and supports the implementation of the National Education Policy.[2]

The 2005 South Asia earthquake – which killed over 73,000 people in Kashmir and the eastern parts of NWFP and resulted in 70,000 with severe injuries or disabilities and 40,000 to 60,000 orphans – had a major effect on education in that part of the country (Asian Development Bank and World Bank, 2005; Rural Development Policy Institute, 2007). Towns and villages were leveled, rendering 3.5 million people homeless, and most of the transportation, education and health infrastructure was destroyed or heavily damaged. Over 18,000 of those who died were students who were crushed in collapsed schools. The education work force was reduced by 60–70% through death, injury or migration (Earthquake Reconstruction and Rehabilitation Authority, 2006).

Conflict and Internal Displacement: Impact on Education

When conflict uproots people, it has a ripple effect on their lives, affecting families' routines and their access to basic services and livelihoods. This was the case in Pakistan where counterinsurgency campaigns beginning in 2008 displaced an estimated 3.3 million people, 80–90% of whom lived with host families and friends or in communal buildings such as schools rather than camps. The IDPs placed a strain on Pakistani infrastructure, with increased demands for health care, sanitation and water in communities witnessing a rapid influx in population in a very short timeframe (UNHCR, 2009).

For various reasons, the 2008–10 crisis forced millions of IDP children and children in host families to miss months of school, with many out of school in 2010. Prior to the conflict, and probably contributing to the vast numbers of IDPs, militant groups attacked hundreds of schools, particularly girls' schools. Other schools were also used as bases by the military, particularly boys' schools (IDMC, 2010b; UN Educational, Scientific and Cultural Organization, 2010). Several months of schooling were missed by IDP children from the main areas of origin, given that their schools were on summer break at the time of displacement and the host community area in the plains were on winter break. In addition, more than 4,500 schools served as shelters for IDPs, especially as they were cooler than tents and had electricity. But they were overcrowded and needed partial or total repair before they could become operational, a process which disrupted the school year once it began in September 2009 (IDMC, 2010b). All schools occupied by IDPs were vacated by the end of August 2009, coinciding with the return of 1.6 million IDPs by around the same date (OCHA, 2009).

While there is a lack of hard data, there are 'strong indications' that internal displacement exposed children to exploitation and abuse (IDMC, 2010b: 4). For example, sexual exploitation of children, particularly boys, also increased during displacement and may be tied to the fact that displacement and the poor economic situation of families drove boys to work. Indeed, child labor, already an issue in Pakistan before the conflict, 'seems to have gone up considerably among displaced children, which may be attributed to the increased poverty and lack of educational opportunities for many of them', according to IDMC (2010b: 22). Child labor was especially likely for displaced boys in child-headed or female-headed households. There are anecdotal reports of internally displaced boys aged three to ten begging, and boys as young as seven were found working in factories or in agriculture. Still others worked in hotels and restaurants, marble quarries and mining facilities, smuggling operations, or temporarily at food hubs or distribution points, carrying food or waiting in lines. (IDMC, 2010b).

According to Save the Children, the government cash grants program for IDPs, issued through debit cards, helped to address child labor issues, perhaps because it helped to alleviate poverty (IDMC, 2010b). While this card system allowed for the distribution of rapid assistance, protection concerns included the following: that assistance was only extended to registered IDPs; some faced technical issues in registering; perceived risks of corruption abounded; distribution was politicized in terms of the selection of beneficiaries; many areas, particularly in FATA, lacked ATMs and electricity; and women may have faced access problems as occurred in food distribution (Cosgrave et al., 2010; UNHCR/Protection Cluster Working Group, 2011).

In terms of other forms of abuse and exploitation, increases in the occurrence of domestic violence, corporal punishment and forced marriage during displacement were also observed. Systematic monitoring and adequate responses by local and international actors to child exploitation and abuse were lacking (IDMC, 2010b). At the same time, it must be noted that there are difficulties even discussing sensitive issues, particularly sexual abuse.

The example of Pakistan reveals that in some cases where the need is so great, humanitarian assistance, despite its good intentions, can have a negative impact on the education children receive. According to an international evaluation of the international humanitarian response to the 2008–10 IDP crisis in Pakistan, interviewees 'complained that the delivery of WFP [World Food Programme] food through government schools was having a big impact on education' (IDMC, 2010b: 53). Delivered to government schools, WFP food rations were said to have driven parents of children attending private schools to put them into the public schools in order to receive the rations. The children pay the price for this switch in the quality of education, as discussed above. Further, girls' dropout rates in government schools are five times greater than that of private schools (Lloyd et al., 2006).

Education in host communities vs. camps

The vast majority of internally displaced children – around 85 to 90% – sought refuge with host communities, particularly in Khyber Pakhtunkhwa (IDMC, 2010b). Families stayed with members of their extended families or with friends or rented rooms. IDP children in host communities were more likely to miss out on schooling than their peers in camps, where IDPs are generally more 'visible' to actors providing education and other services. In some cases, the access to education received in displacement in camps was better than in IDPs' home communities and some IDPs in camps attended school for the first time in their lives (UNICEF, 2009). In contrast, IDP children in host communities generally lacked access to education during displacement. As the Internal Displacement Monitoring Centre (IDMC), which conducted research on the rights of IDP children in northwest Pakistan in February 2010, notes, 'There were serious issues with access to education for internally displaced children in host communities, where demand vastly exceeded availability, particularly during the largest wave of displacement from Swat and

Bunir from April to June 2009' (2010b: 25). Because they were seen as being present in the area only temporarily, internally displaced children were, in some cases, refused admission to schools in host communities. Other schools reported they did not have the resources to provide for displaced children (IDMC, 2010b).

Parental preferences and family considerations affected enrollment. Some parents simply did not want their children, girls in particular, to have to travel the long distances to the schools that were available, or preferred to keep their children close rather than potentially exposing them to further conflict or risk any further emotional trauma. Still other families were uncertain as to the length of their displacement, so did not enroll their children, or were secondarily displaced within host communities or between them and camps. And poverty also kept children out of school, particularly boys as young as seven to work or assist their families by picking up food distributions or other tasks, especially when the fathers left camps and host communities for work (IDMC, 2010b).

In discussing IDPs who seek refuge with families and friends, international actors tend to employ the term 'host communities', casting the receiving communities in a positive or favorable light. But the reality is (not to detract from the generosity of these extended families, friends and other individuals, whose resources were typically already stretched, or the good experiences by IDPs seeking refuge with these communities) that not as much is known about these communities and the conditions faced by IDPs. This contrasts with IDPs in camps who are more accessible by and large to international humanitarian actors. For example, one worrying observation is that IDP girls and boys have served as domestic workers for host families who have taken in their families, with girls in particular remaining with the host family after their family members have returned (IDMC, 2010b).

The massive influx of IDPs made it difficult for host community schools to meet the IDPs' educational needs. Some educational programs were initiated by Pakistani NGOs and community organizations in receiving communities, but they simply could not cater to all IDP children. IDP children in rural or insecure regions were particularly unable to access education, such as in DI Khan and South Waziristan. IDMC identifies four principal reasons impeding displaced children's ability to go to school in host communities: 1. they were not concentrated in a few areas, but were dispersed over many districts; 2. the areas of displacement were largely insecure, with access by aid organizations difficult in many cases as a result; 3. tracking the number of IDPs proved difficult in each subregion so educational need could not be properly assessed; and 4. the Pakistani government may not have sought to focus on educational needs due to its perception that displacement was only temporary (2010b: 25).

In all camps, members of the Education Cluster provided educational opportunities, but between ten and fifteen per cent of children lacked access. Schools lacked teaching materials and adequate staffing, but teachers were found from the camps, within the community and by hiring non-teacher paraprofessionals. According to IDMC, 'approximately 28,000 children in camps were enrolled in school in 2009, mainly at the primary school level. However, coverage for secondary education was much lower' (2010b: 26).

Floods and Internal Displacement: Impact on Education

As with the IDP crisis in 2009, schools served as shelters for many affected by the 2010 floods. By September 2010, almost 3,000 schools and colleges were being used as shelters, accommodating 660,000 people, mostly in Sindh but also in Khyber Pakhtunkhwa (KP) and Balochistan (UN Office for the Coordination of Humanitarian Affairs (OCHA), 2010). The floods strained provincial resources already affected by conflict-induced displacement, as in the case of KP where there were already 1.2 million internally displaced persons (UN General Assembly, 2011).

Education, one of the 12 clusters established by the UN system in the floods response, has not been a central element in the humanitarian response, which has had an impact on children's access to education. The initial Floods Emergency Response Plan, issued in August 2010, sought $459 million for immediate flood relief, revised to $1.9 billion in November 2010. The funding appeal included over 350 project proposals from 153 organizations and was intended to cover 100% of people affected by the disaster in terms of meeting their shelter, health and agriculture needs, 70% of the affected population in terms of food, water, sanitation and hygiene needs and the education needs of only 14% of those affected (Government of Pakistan, National Disaster Management Authority, 2011b). Of the $83.4 million requested for education in the funding appeal (only 4% of the total $1.9 billion requested), only 42% was funded, for partial funding of three of the 22 projects (OCHA, 2011c). The poor funding of the education component of the appeal made it difficult for international agencies to rebuild schools or provide alternative facilities to meet the needs of IDP children for education.

While the UN Children's fund (UNICEF), the UN Educational, Scientific and Cultural Organization (UNESCO) and other international organizations were active in supporting temporary learning centers, it is important to realize that there were and are still significant gaps. These learning centers provided education to only 220,000 children (including 96,000 girls); and more than 400,000 children were enrolled in child-friendly spaces (UN General Assembly, 2011). There were also difficulties in reconciling figures on damaged schools and problems in coordinating educational initiatives between international actors as well as between the government and humanitarian agencies (OCHA, 2010).

At the time of writing, access to education in the aftermath of the 2011 floods is limited, and the general humanitarian situation and longer-term prospects for recovery are worrisome. An estimated 2.7 million of the 5.4 million affected people are children (Tidey, 2011). The floods have had a devastating impact on children and their families, particularly in Sindh, the worst-affected province already hard-hit from the 2010 floods. There has been significant damage in 22 of Sindh's 23 districts (Tidey, 2011). Agricultural output in many districts of Sindh was already devastated by the 2010 floods, with some farmers unable to plant the 2010/2011 spring crop according to the UNDP (UNDP, 2011). Widespread chronic malnutrition persisted at the time of the 2011 floods, after which many have lost a season's harvest. A UNICEF staff member described 'paediatric wards in Sindh's hospitals filled with frighteningly frail children suffering from severe acute malnutrition' (Tidey, 2011) and according to OCHA, there were reports of watery diarrhea, dengue, malaria and acute respiratory infections increasing in the worst-affected districts at the onset of winter (OCHA, 2011b). In addition, 'women's privacy and sense of security is less than before the floods and there are reports of violent incidents against women, boys and girls', with child- and/or women-friendly protective spaces established in flood-affected districts in Sindh, benefitting 41,000 children and 5,000 women, according to OCHA (OCHA, 2011b).

To address the long-term recovery needs of the most vulnerable and marginalized across the flood-affected districts through December 2011, the UN Development Programme (UNDP) and the NDMA launched an early recovery plan for the 2010 floods in April 2011. Sindh is the province most in need and targeted in many of the plan's sectors – agriculture, food security, health and nutrition, education, governance and housing – yet funding shortfalls remain. The education sector required $123 million for 1.3 million beneficiaries, including over 550,000 children in Sindh (UNDP, 2011).

There were 1.8 million people internally displaced by the 2011 floods, around 341,000 of whom were residing in temporary settlements across Sindh as of November 2011. The majority of people in those settlements were women, children, the elderly and the disabled (UNICEF, 2011). Over 5,300 schools were reported as damaged in Sindh, and 90 in Balochistan (OCHA, 2011).

In September 2011, more than 2,400 schools in 10 districts of Sindh continued to host IDPs, according to OCHA, which warned that, 'Voluntary movement of IDPs from these schools needs to be ensured' (OCHA, 2011a). According to UNICEF two months later, 'Indications from the field suggest that many of the displaced people have returned to their home areas to often dismal conditions', including damage or destruction of homes, schools and health clinics, in addition to the loss of crops and livestock (UNICEF, 2011: 1). As of November 2011, some 1,300 temporary learning centers were serving over 65,200 children, with a decline of around 5,000 children 'due to reasons such as population movement and engagement of children in economic activities', and with an overall percentage of 'first timers' of 39% (UNICEF, 2011). As of the same date, UNICEF faced a 70% funding gap for its $50.3 million in programs requested under the Pakistan Rapid Response Fund for the 2011 Floods to meet the immediate needs of children and women for six months and the revision of the response plan was due to occur in late November 2011 (UNICEF, 2011).

Assessing the Government Response to Education in Conflict and Floods

Many of the gaps in education in Pakistan predate the major humanitarian crises of recent years in the country, such as conflict, flooding and the 2005 earthquake. The Pakistani government itself has recognized since its founding as a republic the need to improve access to and the quality of education (Winthrop and Graff, 2010).[3] The government has acknowledged in numerous state reports, policies and in statements its paltry spending on education and its poor indicators in the education sector, including its poor overall literacy rates, among the lowest in South Asia, inadequate infrastructure, wide gender disparity in enrollment and high dropout rates. As stated in its National Education Policy (November 2009), education in Pakistan is marked with 'significant quality deficits', which the policy seeks to reform, including in terms of teachers and pedagogy, curriculum and textbooks among other inputs. The 2009 National Education Policy also admits and seeks to overcome the 'relative failure of the State's educational system' which the government sees as a factor contributing to the emergence of private schools and madrasas which have 'created unequal opportunities for students' (Government of Pakistan, Ministry of Education, 2009, sections 5.5.104, 1.3.18 and 3.5.72).

The inclusion of 'education in emergencies' and related policy actions set forth in Pakistan's latest 2009 education policy, adopted months after the 2009 IDP crisis, marks a positive step forward on the part of the government. The policy recognizes that the country's educational system has been ill-prepared and hit by large-scale emergencies since the 2005 earthquake. The policy sets forth that improvements shall be made not only to the physical school infra-structure to bring it into line with international standards, but also in terms of governance; increasing student awareness for dealing with crisis situa-tions; teacher education; the incorporation of topics related to crises, natural disasters, trauma management and crisis response into the curriculum; and other measures. While these advances in the latest national education policy are to be lauded, it remains to be seen if its measures can be translated from rhetoric to effective practice.

At provincial or district levels, simple policies can be adopted to facilitate educational access. Under a directive issued by the Khyber Pakhtunkhwa Ministry of Education in response to the 2009 IDP crisis, school principals were obliged to admit students regardless of documentation. Such measures proved successful in some cases, such as in Mardan and Charsadda, following advocacy on this directive by aid providers. But registration in KP was hindered by inadequate infrastructure to cater to IDPs (IDMC, 2010b). In host communities in Bajaur agency in 2008, many positive measures were taken to increase IDPs' access to education, but were often marred by various problems. For example, IDP teachers taught IDP children; schools ran in double shifts, with IDP children segregated from host community children so as to minimize disruption; the government sought to deputize host community teachers; paraprofessionals lacking formal teaching qualifications were hired, but their other qualifications 'varied widely'; and teacher salaries were increased but they faced heavy workloads (IDMC, 2010b). Many of these measures were implemented to respond to the rapid and larger influx of IDPs from Swat and Bunir in 2009, but local resources were too overwhelmed to provide an adequate response (IDMC, 2010b). It is also important to ensure at the district level that children receive certificates for education received in displacement. In some cases, despite efforts by schools to facilitate certification with district officials, families returned home too quickly (IDMC, 2010b). Procedures should be developed to ensure that children receive credit for the education they receive while displaced.

The sheer scale of the 2010 floods overwhelmed government capacity; indeed, 'no government could have managed alone' in the words of the UN Secretary-General (UN General Assembly, 2011: 3). The government's National Disaster Management Authority (NDMA), in its 'lessons learned' paper, acknowledged that there was a lack of capacity at the provincial level, particularly in Punjab and Sindh where there was little experience with disaster management. The situation was much better in Khyber Pakhtunkhwa because of its recent experience with humanitarian catastrophes. At the national level, the NDMA team at the time the floods began had only 21 staff; requests to other government ministries, with the exception of the Defense Forces, to second staff were not very successful. A number of national and international NGOs had established networks, warehouses and systems for disaster response there while such systems were almost non-existent in Punjab and Sindh (2011a).

Conclusion

In a country where educational indicators are low and the government has not prioritized education for its citizens, it is perhaps not surprising that when conflict and disasters occur, displaced children have experienced serious shortcomings in accessing education. But difficulties in ensuring schooling for children during and after displacement are also a product of the government seeing displacement as temporary, insecurity, problems in coordination between international organizations and the government, and some donors preferring to support life-saving interventions.

As this chapter has revealed, more attention needs to be paid to ensuring that internally displaced children in Pakistan have access to quality education. With millions affected by emergencies in Pakistan, the majority of whom are children, improved monitoring and data collection are needed for a proper assessment of the impact of disasters and conflict, including over the long-term, on education. Displacement due to disasters and conflict and extended periods out of school, in addition to inadequate psychosocial assistance to affected children and young people, can have marked and long-lasting effects on displaced children. At the same time, in some cases children may have access to education in displacement for the first time, only to be bereft of it once again upon return to their home communities. For these reasons, the government and international community need to exhibit greater will and commit greater resources to community preparedness and prevention measures as well as to emergency, early recovery and development programs which prioritize education, in order to ensure that crises do not irreparably jeopardize the education of children and young people in Pakistan. Certainly the children and young people of Pakistan should not continue to bear the burden for the lack of investment in these critical measures.

Questions for Further Discussion

Given the various issues and constraints discussed herein, what are the most effective measures that the government – particularly at the provincial and district levels – international organizations and Pakistani NGOs can take to ensure access to quality education for IDP children?

To what extent do the temporary learning centers and other education interventions provide access to quality education in Pakistan? What are some good practices and what is needed to overcome any barriers?

What are the psychosocial needs of children affected by conflict and disasters in Pakistan? To what extent are they being addressed?

What expectations do IDP and returnee families have for their children's education and how are these being addressed?

Notes

1 The Internal Displacement Monitoring Centre (IDMC) estimates that 3.35 million people were displaced between 2008 and May 2010; UNICEF reported that more than 60% of the displaced population in Pakistan was under the age of 18.
2 See the Pakistan Education Task Force Web site (pakistaneducationtask-force.com/index.html).

3 For example, Pakistan set forth a plan in 1956 which set the goal of achieving universal primary education by 1961. Free and compulsory education for all children is guaranteed in the 1973 Constitution and subsequent constitutional reforms. In addition, some 35 government reports between 1959 and 1993 have recognized the shortcomings in the quality of school examinations.

References

Andrabi, T., Das, J. and Khwaja, A., (2002), *The rise of private schooling in Pakistan: Catering to the urban elite or educating the rural poor?* economics-files.pomona.edu/Andrabi/Research/Pakschool%20March29.pdf

Asian Development Bank and World Bank, (2010a), 'ADB-WB Assess Pakistan Flood Damage at $9.7 Billion,' Press Release No. 2011/134/SAR, 14 October 2010 web.worldbank.org/WBSITE/EXTERNAL/NEWS/0,,contentMDK:22733998~pagePK:64257043~piPK:437376~theSitePK:4607,00.html (Accessed 10 October 2011).

—(2010b), '*Pakistan floods 2010: Preliminary damage and needs assessment* www.worldbank.org.pk/WBSITE/EXTERNAL/COUNTRIES/SOUTHASIAEXT/PAKISTANEXTN/0,,contentMDK:22797764~menuPK:50003484~pagePK:2865066~piPK:2865079~theSitePK:293052,00.html (Accessed 10 October 2011).

Das, J. and Andrabi, T., (2010), 'Private schools, earthquakes: What we know from Pakistan (with insights for Haiti),' Power Point, presented at the 54th annual conference of the Comparative and International Education Society in Chicago, IL on March 3rd 2010. www.leapsproject.org/site/publications (Accessed 10 October 2011).

Earthquake Reconstruction and Rehabilitation Authority (ERRA) (2006), *Annual Review 2005 to 2006.*

Government of Pakistan, Federal Bureau of Statistics, (2010), *Pakistan social and living standards measurement survey (PSLM 2008–2009)*, section 2.5. www.statpak.gov.pk/fbs/content/pakistan-social-and-living-standards-measurement-survey-pslm-2008-09-provincial-district (Accessed 15 October 2011).

Government of Pakistan, Ministry of Education, (2009), National education policy 2009, November 2009. www.infopak.gov.pk/National_Education_Policy_2009.pdf (Accessed 15 October 2011).

Government of Pakistan, National Disaster Management Authority (NDMA), (2011)a, *Pakistan 2010 flood relief: learning from experience.* reliefweb.int/node/399243 (Accessed 15 October 2011).

—(2011b), *A review of the Pakistan flood relief and early recovery response plan (PFRERRP) up to December 31, (2010)* www.pakresponse.info/LinkClick.aspx?fileticket=SDfwX0k4v-s%3D&tabid=73&mid =440 (Accessed 15 October 2011).

Internal Displacement Monitoring Centre (IDMC), 2010a, *Internal displacement: Global overview of trends and developments in 2009*, p. 13. www.internal-displacement.org (Accessed 25 October 2011).

—(2010b), *Still at risk: Internally displaced children's rights in north-west Pakistan.* www.internal-displacement.org.

—(2009), *Pakistan: millions of IDPs and returnees face continuing crisis: A profile of the internal displacement situation*. www.internal-displacement.org (Accessed 15 October 2011)

International Crisis Group, 2007, *Pakistan: The forgotten conflict in Balochistan*, Asia Briefing no. 60. www.crisisgroup.org (Accessed 5 October 2011).

Lloyd, C., Mete, C. and Grant, M., (2006), *The implications of changing educational and family circumstances for children's grade progression in rural Pakistan: 1997–2004*, Policy Research Division Working Paper No. 209, pp. 13 and 28 (New York: Population Council. www.popcouncil.org/pdfs/wp/209.pdf (Accessed 15 October 2011).

OCHA, (2010), 29 September 2010, *Pakistan: Monsoon floods: Situation report no. 28*. reliefweb.int/node/369502

—(2011a), *Pakistan Humanitarian Bulletin 29 September 2011*.

—(2011b), *Pakistan: Monsoon 2011: Situation report no. 11*, 4 November 2011. reliefweb.int/node/457356

—Financial Tracking Service, (2011c), *Flash Appeal: Pakistan Floods Relief and Early Recovery Response Plan (Revised) (August 2010 – July 2011), Table E: List of Appeal Projects (grouped by sector), with funding status of each Report as of 06-November-2011*. floods2010.pakresponse.info/Funding/PakistanFloodsEmergencyResponsePlan2010.aspx

Oxfam, (2011), *Six months into the floods: Resetting Pakistan's priorities through reconstruction*. www.oxfam.org)

Pakistan Education Task Force, (2011), *Emergency Education: Pakistan*. pakistaneducationtaskforce.com/EER.html (Accessed 5 October 2011).

Polastro, R., Nagrah, A., Steen, N. and Zafar, F., (2011), *Inter-agency real time evaluation (IARTE) of the humanitarian response to Pakistan's 2010 flood crisis* (Geneva: DARA). daraint.org (Accessed 5 October 2011).

Rural Development Policy Institute, (2007), 'Pakistan: Earthquake orphans still wait for the re-integration strategy'. reliefweb.int/sites/reliefweb.int/files/reliefweb_pdf/node-235147.pdf (Accessed 15 October 2011).

South Asian Forum for Education Development, (2011), *Annual status of education report 2010*. www.safedafed.org (Accessed 15 November 2011).

Tidey, C., (2011), 'Pakistan's floods throw the need for disaster preparation into stark relief', Poverty Matters Blog, *The Guardian*, 4 November 2011. www.guardian.co.uk/global-development/poverty-matters/2011/nov/04/pakistan-floods-lessons-risk-reduction (Accessed 15 December 2011).

UN Children's Fund (UNICEF), *Internally displaced people in Pakistan*, 2009. www.unicef.org/pakistan/overview_5981.htm (Accessed 15 November 2011).

UNICEF, (2011), *UNICEF Pakistan Update: 2011 Floods: Needs and Response*, dated 2 November 2011 and filed as 4 November 2011 in OCHA Pakistan Web site. pakresponse.info) (Accessed 15 January 2012).

UN Commission on Human Rights, (1998), Guiding principles on internal displacement, UN doc. E/CN.4/1998/53/Add.2. www.brookings.edu/projects/idp/gp_page.aspx (Accessed 15 October 2011).

UN Development Programme (UNDP), (2011), 'Snapshot for Gap Analysis in Agriculture', 'Snapshot for Gap Analysis in Food Security', 'Snapshot of Gap Analysis for Early Recovery in Health and Nutrition', Snapshot of Gap Analysis for Early Recovery in Governance', 'Snapshot of Gap Analysis for Early Recovery in Housing', and 'Snapshot for Gap Analysis in Education', in *Strategic Early Recovery Action Plan – at a glance.* floods2010.pakresponse.info/LinkClick.aspx?fileticket=BAOUzi-72kA%3d&tabid=40&mid=1344 (Accessed 15 January 2012).

UN Educational, Scientific and Cultural Organization (UNESCO), (2010), *Education under attack 2010*, pp. 215–9 (unesdoc.unesco.org/images/0018/001868/186809e.pdfSimilar) (Accessed 15 October 2011).

UN General Assembly, (2011), *Strengthening emergency relief, rehabilitation, reconstruction and prevention in the wake of devastating floods in Pakistan: Report of the Secretary-General*, UN doc. A/65/773. www.un.org/ga/search/view_doc.asp?symbol=A/65/773 (Accessed 5 October 2011).

UN High Commissioner for Refugees (UNHCR), (10 June 2009), 'More and more Pakistani displaced move to camps as needs grow'. www.alertnet.org/thenews/newsdesk/UNHCR/08f1a477c986fb1c1c29c331c17caa95.htm (Accessed 15 October 2011).

UNHCR/Protection Cluster Working Group, (2011), *The WATAN scheme for flood relief: Protection highlights 2010–2011*. floods2010.pakresponse.info/WorkingGroups/Protection.aspx (Accessed 12 November 2011).

UN Office for the Coordination of Humanitarian Affairs (OCHA), 28 August 2009, *Pakistan situation report no. 15*. reliefweb.int/node/322152 (Accessed 15 October 2011).

United States Agency for International Development, (30 November 2010), *Pakistan floods fact sheet no. 7, fiscal year 2011*. www.usaid.gov/our_work/humanitarian_assistance/disaster_assistance/countries/pakistan/template/fs_sr/fy2011/pakistan_fl_fs07_11-30-2010.pdf (Accessed 15 October 2011).

Winthrop, R. and Graff, C., (2010), *Beyond madrasas: Assessing the links between education and militancy in Pakistan*, Center for Universal Education, Working Paper 2. www.brookings.edu/papers/.../06_pakistan_education_winthrop.aspxCached – Similar (Accessed 25 October 2011).

The Challenges for Education of Protracted Displacement in Sri Lanka

6

Lynn Davies

Chapter Outline

Abstract

In this chapter, the historical and contemporary situation of internally displaced persons in Sri Lanka is outlined, before critically examining government policy on displacement and return. The particular impacts on children and young people, and on their education, are detailed, and current strategies with regard to educational provision for IDPs analysed, including consideration of the research base to strategy. Three critical theoretical analyses are generated by this discussion: the question of 'hosts', the political economy surrounding displacement and discrimination, and the relation of IDP education to peacebuilding.

Introduction

This chapter outlines the historical and contemporary situation with regard to Internally Displaced Persons (IDPs) in Sri Lanka and critically examines current government policy on displacement and return. Ongoing strategies by a range of actors with regard to educational provision for IDPs and returnees can then be examined in the light of this. The sources for data for this discussion come mainly from international NGOs or agencies, or from personal testimony of IDPs, as well as from a growing number of research studies. Visits by the author over a number of years have enabled some insights. The context of displacement in Sri Lanka has also generated some critical theoretical analyses, namely the question of 'hosts', the political economy surrounding discrimination and displacement, and the relation of IDP education to peacebuilding.

Background and History

Sri Lanka has a long history of internal conflict as well as of natural disasters. The 26-year-old conflict between the Sinhalese dominated government and the separatist LTTE[1] ended officially in 2009 with a military victory. The long protracted struggle has left thousands of IDPs from, as well as in, the North and East of Sri Lanka. Figures vary and have changed significantly each year of the conflict, with new displacements as well as new returnees. In late 2010, over 320,000 people who had fled their homes due to the armed conflict before and after the military push of 2008 were estimated to remain internally displaced (OCHA, 2011a). It is also estimated that 230,000 internally displaced persons still need humanitarian assistance (OCHA, 2011b).

An early and major cause of displacement was the forced eviction of the north-Eastern Muslims by the LTTE in October 1990, often referred to as 'ethnic cleansing'. The Muslims were a minority in the Northern Province, but coexisted well with the majority Tamils, with similarities in language and culture. Yet there were differences in political views and the emergence of an exclusive political party for the Muslims in the Eastern Province reflected this. Muslims were ordered to leave their homes within 24 hours, later extended to 48 hours. A population of 75,000 men, women and children left the area. About 65,000 arrived in the district of Puttalam and were accommodated in welfare centres in predominantly Muslim divisions, in nearly 200 different locations. Others came later after being displaced more than once in various parts of the country. Initially they maintained distinctions between local and IDP Muslims, and constructed identities around their place of origin. There were cultural differences: in some areas of the North, Muslim women had more freedom in that they could move freely and pursue education (the influence of which served to create some cultural adaptation in the host community regarding the aspirations of women). Initially IDPs were welcomed by the hosts, sharing resources such as schools, but then with protracted displacement, relationships deteriorated. IDPs strained the local economy, and the oversupply of labour drove wages down. Humanitarian interventions that were focussed only on IDPs caused resentment in the poorer sections of the host community. Currently, the question is of return or (re)integration. Intermediate generations had memories of their villages, but saw that their lives were tied to those of their children who had settled in Puttalam. With every year, the reversal of ethnic cleansing becomes more difficult. It was felt mostly that there was now unity and brotherhood with the host community (Badurdeen, 2010).

The tsunami of December 2004 led to 35,000 tsunami-related deaths and initial displacement of about one million people. The North and East were especially badly hit, registering about 55% of deaths and 65% of initial displacements together with 60% of the damage (Chapman et al., 2009). Several strategies from donors (e.g. World Bank, Asian Development Bank, UN, EC) featured resettlement and reintegration, with land and housing support. There has however been some resentment that those displaced by the tsunami received more support than those displaced by conflict (Cohen 2008).

After the abrogation of the cease-fire agreement (CFA) between the Government of Sri Lanka (GoSL) and the LTTE in January 2008, the government intensified the war in LTTE-controlled areas. The ensuing fluidity of the military situation resulted in the frequent and unexpected displacement of citizens and the rapid deterioration of public institutions and facilities in the conflict areas (UNICEF, 2010). Children were particularly vulnerable under these conditions. The period generated over 280,000 IDPs, adding to the existing case-load of nearly 300,000 IDPs. Among people who had fled their homes prior to April 2008 ('old' IDPs), at least 227,000 remained in displacement.

Government Policy and its Impact

The Report of the Representative of the Secretary General of the Human Rights of Internally Displaced Persons states that '*as citizens of their country, IDPs in Sri Lanka remain entitled to all guarantees of international human rights and international humanitarian law subscribed to by the State or applicable as customary-international law*' (reported in Badurdeen, 2010). This presumably includes the right to education.[2]

However, as pointed out by UNESCO (2011), in contrast to refugees, there is no international legally binding agreement regarding the rights of IDPs. Responsibility for protecting and assisting IDPs lies with national authorities, which is problematic in countries such as Sri Lanka where governments are implicated in displacements. Many countries with large internally displaced populations have failed to develop rules and practices to protect education, and Sri Lanka would be no exception.

Not only are there failures in policy, there continue to be severe implications of government strategy. Even after 2009, military spending remained a priority in the government's budget, with only a small amount of money allocated to supporting IDPs and returnees (OCHA, 2011a). At the same time, humanitarian agencies providing assistance and protection were faced with both funding shortages and access restrictions. The financial shortfalls during 2010 may have been due to the reluctance on the part of international donors to fund programmes that were dependent on short-term approval of government and could be called off at short notice. The massive camps were closed sites, where local authorities took sole responsibility for managing schooling, but where any form of community involvement was prohibited. There was no access for teacher training or monitoring (Williams, 2010). It was problematic that the GoSL did not endorse the UN's Common Humanitarian Action Plan (CHAP) for 2010 (IDRC, 2011a).

Questions remain of whether the government is now neglecting the long-term displaced in favour of the recent influx of IDPs during the last phase of the war. The northern Muslim IDP situation has been highly politicized, with politicians manipulating the aggrieved context and using it for their benefit as a potential voter base. In spite of promises in 2009, no plan has yet been finalized and no structures put in place that would differentiate between the needs of the long-term displaced and the short-term displaced (Haniffa, 2011). Haniffa reports on the launch on 3 November 2011 of the Citizens' Commission on the expulsion of Muslims from the Northern province in 1990, claiming that The LTTE expulsion of Muslims has not been adequately integrated into any mainstream historical narrative in Sri Lanka. The Commission has heard that the northern Muslims need assistance to return, and that due to lack of transport to school and poor facilities, children are dropping out.

Although the civil war is officially over, there are still significant horizontal inequalities, with claims that the government is favouring Sinhalese settlers in prime areas for relocation (Shankar, 2009). The problems of managing IDP populations are heightened by the continued existence of the controversial High Security Zones (HSZs) preventing IDPs from returning to their homes or pursuing their usual forms of livelihood. The HSZ zones have displaced almost 130,000 people, who have to live with relatives or in camps. Many were from farming or fishing communities and a deep cultural tradition underlies this controversy, as people seek to preserve their original land and land rights. Over 100 complaints had been lodged with the Human Rights Commission, asserting that HSZs violate fundamental and constitutional rights (Shankar, 2009).

Other sorts of categorization and segregation also remain problematic. During the months after the end of the conflict, the Sri Lankan Army (SLA) and two police investigation divisions screened the 'new' IDP population and separated several thousand adults from the IDPs because of their alleged association with the LTTE. The exact process of the screening of 'separatees' remains unclear, as did the criteria for detention and release as well as the modalities of 'rehabilitation' (OCHA, 2011a). They were not formally charged. All this would generate additional trauma for their families and children.

Another category is 'surrendees', identified at the end of the conflict as formerly associated with armed groups. On 25 May 2010, all 567 'surrendee' children and young people, including 201 girls, were released, upon completion of one year of rehabilitation as required by Emergency Regulation No. 1580/5 (2008). In line with Regulation 1580/5, monitoring of these children is ongoing by the Department of Probation and Child Care Services. In addition to highlighting the limited employment opportunities, the monitoring showed that at least 250 children formerly associated with armed groups in the north and east of the country are facing a number of security issues. Concerns range from being requested to report regularly to the nearby military/police posts, visits by military and police/intelligence staff to their house and arrests by the police, to being required to report and sign in at the local military or navy post before leaving their administrative division of residence (UN SRCAC, 2011).

In May 2010 President Rajapaksa appointed a Lessons Learned and Reconciliation Commission (LLRC) to report on the armed conflict during the period from February 2002 to May 2009. The LLRC received criticism for its mandate, which did not include an investigation into war crimes committed by either side, for its lack of independence and for its lack of witness protection (OCHA, 2011a).

Conflict and Educational Provision

The issue of education and displacement has to be set within the picture of education in Sri Lanka as a whole as well as of education in the conflict-affected areas. The Sri Lankan education system overall is described as 'strong' with a national Ministry of Education, which is then decentralized into nine provinces, each province then divided into zones. Although the structure is relatively well-staffed, financing for education remains a challenge (Papadopolous, 2010). There is a high literacy rate and high enrolment rate in the Central and South areas. Even during the conflict, in affected areas cease-fires would be called and respected during times of national exams (Williams, 2010). The conflict-affected areas however experienced significant human resource constraints, poor allocation of funding and a lack of materials and infrastructure. These areas were seen as neglected and not prioritized by the government (Papadopolous, 2010). This was part of the grievance by the LTTE.

During the conflict, schools in the North and East were badly affected. Schools themselves were turned into IDP camps and became military targets. In 2006 and 2007 both parties to the conflict attacked schools. Shelling by the military destroyed schools and resulted in the death and injury of students and teachers, sometimes in response to alleged LTTE shelling from the area (O'Malley, 2010). It was not just schools that were affected, but also teacher training provision: professional centres for teachers, such as the Distant Education Centre, Postgraduate Diploma in Education Centres and the Bachelor of Education Centres are now reported as defunct (Thambiah, 2011).

The organization *Peace Women* reported in May 2011 that schools are still in use as barracks for the Sri Lankan security forces, and as a transit site for IDPs who have left IDP camps but cannot yet return to their place of origin because of landmines. (Tamil News, 2011). A different newspaper report quotes a UNICEF official stating that Government funds are mainly used to pay teachers' and education officials' salaries; a minimal amount goes towards rehabilitating school buildings and providing teaching materials (Irin News,

2011). The political situation with regard to government policy is returned to in the final section.

Children, Displacement and Schooling

Children who are displaced are part of a larger category of what *Save The Children Sri Lanka* refer to as 'Children on the Move' (2010). These include children who have been trafficked, children who migrate (e.g. to pursue better life opportunities, look for work or education or to escape exploitative or abusive situations at home); children displaced by conflict and natural disasters; and children who live and work in the streets. All these children are considered as a vulnerable category in need of care and protection. Save The Children also distinguish different types of displacement: those displaced by conflict, those displaced by human-elephant conflict and development-induced displacement. Children may migrate to other areas for educational purposes (De Silva and Punchihewa, 2010).

Abduction might be seen as a particular form of displacement. In 2007, fear of abduction en route to school for recruitment into armed groups led some parents in IDP camps to keep their children from school. The LTTE had forcibly recruited children on their way to or from school and in the past had used schools as voluntary recruitment sites. In May 2009, children as young as nine years old were abducted from camps for Tamil IDPs in northern Sri Lanka. Some were taken for ransom and others were abducted by paramilitaries for questioning over links to the rebel movement. The UN found strong evidence of security forces sometimes supporting or participating in the abduction and forced recruitment of child soldiers by the Karuna group (O'Malley, 2010).

With the volatile situation in Sri Lanka, and the different types of displacement, it is difficult to calculate absolute figures for the number of displaced children who are or who are not in school. Ferris and Winthrop (2010) report that enrolment rates of primary-age IDP children are high compared to other countries with significant displaced populations. Only three per cent of primary-age children are out of school in the country altogether, although one assumes that the proportion would be higher for IDPs. Using the assumption of one-third of IDPs being of school age, this gives a figure of 126,667 school-age IDPs (out of 380,000). Ferris and Winthrop do not specify how many of these would be out of school, primary or secondary, and presumably this would be not a static figure at all. UNICEF (2010) however are able to state that in total approximately 80,000 students, representing 95% of the school-aged population (5–14 years), attended schools in IDP camps. What we do not know of course is how 'solid' this attendance is.

In considering education and IDPs, it is clearly important to include not just the children who are displaced, but those in families who have returned to their own or other sites for relocation. This raises questions of (re)integration. Educational concerns affect a much larger population than those still labelled IDP.

Impact of Displacement on Education

This section turns to the various pictures of the impact of displacement on education. Much depends clearly on whether children are in 'temporary' schools in camps, or living with relatives and host families and attending normal schools or living almost permanently as communities in 'host' districts. Humanitarian agencies noticed that some IDPs resisted registering their children in local schools, fearing this would make their displacement seem permanent (Williams, 2010). Whether they are – or perceive themselves to be – long-stay or short-stay is then another obvious variable, as is whether they go back to schools which continued to function or those that closed and were then 'restarted'. Whatever the situation, testimony shows an intricate set of problems, and this section merely provides some illustrations.

In 2005–6, for example, talking to IDPs as part of the US Brookings-Bern project on internal displacement revealed constant concerns about education (Cohen, 2008). Parents complained about safety and transportation problems because there was no school nearby, also revealing gender issues:

> 'Our children have to walk more than six km or have to hire an auto. We don't have enough bus services. Because of that reason our girls can't continue their education.'

Another mother said,

> 'Every day school teachers are asking for money. That is also the main barrier to continue children's education.' (Cohen, 2008: 21)

With regard to poverty, one girl similarly recounted to the Lessons Learned and Reconciliation Commission in 2008:

'My family lost everything due to displacement. My parents managed to send me to school in Puttalam, and I have finished my education. But most parents found it difficult to let their children continue their education. Because they were pushed to poverty after displacement; forced to stay in camps; and they were jobless; and could not afford to send their children to school' (Groundviews, 2008).

An IDP student in a camp was quoted in a Save The Children report:

'It is difficult to study there. We live in tents. The floor is uneven. I can't study or do homework there. My old school was much better' (Save The Children, 2009).

Even after years of displacement, the educational situation remains grave. The Internal Displacement Monitoring Centre (IDMC) reported in January 2011 that physical infrastructure for schools was still lacking and there was a lack of teachers in the camps as well as in the return areas. Government spending in the education sector remained low compared to other countries in South Asia. In January 2010 there were only 300 teachers for more than 23,000 pupils in the Menik Farm camp (IDMC, 2011b). Volunteer teachers lacked teaching experience. Children's education was disrupted each year during the monsoon season because Temporary Learning Spaces were used as rain shelters (IDMC, 2011a). Because of the lack of teachers, in Menik Farm some families sent their children to children's homes in Vavuniya to give them access to education (which would be a further displacement). OCHA reported in 2010 that despite free transport services from Vavuniya to Menik Farm, teacher absenteeism and hence a lack of teachers continued to jeopardize education services for students still in the camp. Williams (2010) raised an interesting point about the type of education in the camps: non-formal approaches might have been better suited to the situation, but NGOs were barred from providing such services:

'Consequently teaching would rigidly adhere to the national curriculum and be managed by education officials among the residents, overseen by the Zonal Education Department. This lack of flexibility meant that the 'education' on offer could not meet the standards of appropriacy, relevance, participation, inclusivity and protection that children who had experienced such dislocation and trauma needed' (Williams, 2010: 4).

On the other hand, it might be argued that the national curriculum would represent 'normality' and would be welcomed by residents as suitable preparation for exams and for higher education. Hurwit (2011) recounts the same problems of IDP education in Sri Lanka as raised generally by the Brookings-Bern project on internal displacement, including infrastructure and discrimination but also material concerns such as children not having the necessary school supplies. At the age of 14, when compulsory schooling ends, children often drop out so as to alleviate the economic burden facing their families. Higher studies require commitment and often private tuition. In particular Hurwit talks of the problem of English education for IDPs, which is often a prerequisite for salaried jobs in a globalized society.

This last comment goes back to the earlier mention of education in Sri Lanka being a normal and prized feature for the vast majority of children, and parents having high aspirations. The Brookings-Bern project found that a major concern for IDP families in Sri Lanka was their children's education. During the 2008 flight, communities' commitment to protecting the right to education was seen. Tractors were loaded with school equipment, children sat in classes under trees or tarpaulins, often in the grounds of host schools, studying while their families arranged shelter, food and water (Williams, 2010). Yet an international NGO converted the one empty room at the camp into a play area rather than a reading room where the children could study and do their homework. 'They never asked us,' IDP families told a visiting delegation: 'if they had, they would have known that we wanted a study room.' One humanitarian expert put it well, 'Perhaps aid workers need smaller mouths and bigger ears.' (Cohen, 2008: 1)

A different situation from that in the camps, and what residents would want there, was found for those displaced persons who relocated to communities, or 'hosts'. Many interviewees in Badurdeen's (2010) study of long term IDPs in Puttalam claimed that there were no disparities in schools for their children, that they were treated equally. The lack of infrastructure was a common problem for both. In fact, schools became important avenues to build relationships between IDPs and host children. FLICT[3] reported that one of the main areas considered for conflict transformation projects was the school system in Puttalam (2006). Yet other reports to the LLRC (Groundviews, 2008) were less sanguine. There, respondents said that the children who were displaced had to face discrimination in schools. 'I was not allowed to take part in any sports or extra-curricular activities. Our talents were wasted.' A submission in November 2010 said that the host community felt the IDPs were infringing on the local university entrance quota.

This relates to the status of IDPs within a new community. In Sri Lanka,

IDPs objected to being considered outsiders rather than citizens. One IDP complained:

> 'Some people look at us and call us refugees. We have to face this type of experience in public places such as in the market, the lake and also in the public sector…' (Cohen, 2008: 9).

Losing citizen identity and claims to basic rights such as education is an extremely harrowing part of displacement. A UNICEF Education chief (quoted in Williams, 2010) noted a sense of order and purpose in camps where schooling had been established. But what was lacking was education as defined by the Convention on the Rights of the Child: respect for rights and fundamental freedoms and respect for cultural identity, language and values. Education for citizenship would not be apparent here.

Return

The eventual and highly significant aspect of being a displaced citizen and displaced family is the question of when – or whether – to return, and what is returned to. A submission to the LLRC described how in terms of return to the conflict-affected areas, the schools were functioning but there were problems of transport and roads and not enough facilities for those returning. Tamils were asking 'why did you come back?' Yet returnees would like their children to take advantage of the low cut-off mark for university entrance in certain sections of the Northern Province, and wanted to benefit from the development activities there (Cohen, 2008). It is a highly strategic as well as emotional decision.

In 2011, IDRC report that progress is being made in making education available in 'return areas' in the North and East, but obstacles remain. By October 2010, 226 schools had reopened out of a total of 326, with more than 40,000 pupils enrolled – yet this was half the figure (82,000) recorded in 2008. The low attendance was reported to be because of problems such as issues of transport, children staying on in host schools or students helping their parents with livelihood activities. More than 600 teachers were still needed.

Some primary and secondary schools continue to be occupied by government forces or used as detention or 'rehabilitation' sites for 'separatees'. Some schools are being used simultaneously as a separate site and as a school. From UNOCHA sources, IDRC report that this sharing has had a negative effect on children's education. Girls in particular did not want to use the shared toilets, and infrastructure, including water, was being diverted from the school to the separate site. In addition, schools that had been occupied by military forces were reported to remain damaged, with little or no reconstruction of their infrastructure after occupation ended.

Identity and Documentation

Whether still displaced or as returnees, the often brutal process of displacement can mean the loss of vital documents that show identity and history. It was reported that trying to retrieve documents or access the source of registration could mean having to return to dangerous areas of origin. An IDP woman explained:

> 'Most of the people don't have a birth certificate and identity card. We tried many times but still couldn't obtain these because our registration is still in the north where it is too dangerous to go'. (Cohen, 2009: 14).

Lack of proof of identity, such as a birth certificate, can lead to discrimination in schools (de Silva and Puchihewa, 2010)

There are currently newspaper reports of a 'gridlock' in Northern Education, with students and teachers facing administration problems as most of their educational documents have been destroyed. Students have lost Ordinary and Advanced level results and school-leaving certificates. Students in war-affected areas could not sit for their OL exams in January 2009, sitting in December 2009, but the results have still not been released. Students have lost a year of their A levels. There are complaints by the Educationist Organisation of Tamils (EOT) about the lack of serious attention to all these issues at zonal and provincial levels (Thambiah, 2011). Schools have lost log books, admissions registers, inventory books and financial statements. Principals and teachers are unable to receive promotions because they cannot produce leave records and submit extracts from their log books regarding the assumption of duties. Pensions are affected. What happens from all this is increased grievances of students and teachers, which does not help social stability and is likely to lead to more disruption and protest.

Yet again, disparities in opportunities between the conflict affected areas and the rest of the country will continue and even be compounded.

Research on Impact on Learners

As was seen above, much of the writing on displacement constitutes either descriptive and numerical data on schools or teachers, or personal testimony. This section examines the extent of focussed research studies on the impact – psychosocial and hence academic – on learners. Receptivity to learning is clearly compromised. Many children have been displaced numerous times, from both natural and man-made disasters. They live with constant uncertainty as well as impoverished conditions, with few recreational facilities. Studies show a social and psychological impact (Fonseka and Cassiere-Daniel, 2009), with children experiencing breakdowns in social relationships and networks as well as fear and anxiety. Children have been found to have limited or no hopes for the future, an inability to plan, as well as to exhibit mental strain and behavioural changes. Fonseka and Cassiere-Daniel however draw attention to the dearth of information and attention on children in displacement. They state that none of the existing national laws or policies which are relevant to children deals with this specific issue of displaced children, and claim that while there are studies on the IDP situation in Sri Lanka, there is no available information on the protection and care needs of children who have been recently displaced. Significantly, in their study they found that children found happiness for the most part in school and school-related activities, play and recreational activities and family. Yet as residents from villages and unfamiliar with town settings, girls in particular were vulnerable to abuse. The argument is that authorities should have an adequate legal and policy framework in place to ensure that rights of children in displacement and their protection needs are adequately addressed.

Lack of knowledge about mental health conditions is confirmed by a survey in Jaffna by Husain et al. (2011). Again, they cite few previous studies in this area. There was no national baseline data with which to compare their findings. One interesting finding from previous studies was that the severity of a mental health condition is reduced during protracted war situations as communities learn to develop 'survival skills'; yet they found the recent experience of those in IDP camps would mean a different reaction. Mental health problems affected up to one-third of participants and almost half those living in IDP camps. Women were particularly prone to depression and anxiety, as were those of older age. However, those in the 15–17 age group experienced significantly less post-traumatic stress disorder (PTSD), anxiety and depression than those in older age groups. This could be hypothesized as linked to less experience of multiple trauma, as well as fewer current concerns about employment, finance and taking care of the needs of families.

It is argued that government authorities appeared to pay little attention to people's psychosocial needs after the war (Hellmann-Rajanayagam, 2010); this gap is being filled by organizations such as GIZ with the Psycho Social Care, Guidance and Counselling component of their *Education for Social Cohesion* programme. In an interview[4] the Secretary of Education, Northern Province said that he saw misbehaviour in his schools as a problem, with vandalism and fighting between pupils, as well as the issues of the dress of girls. Students had spent months in the camps, and there was no livelihood for parents in the resettlement areas. In this area, counsellors identify three groups: those who have lost parents in the war, those who are scared of their new life or have intrusive memories of the war, and those who are being sexually harassed or abused. One aim of the psychosocial initiatives is to break the cycle of violence. It is culturally accepted for children (and wives) to be beaten in the home, and one effect of war has been to make people not think about this – there is greater violence out there. Another cultural question is that there are very few women counsellors for areas which include IDPs, as the women are seen to 'refuse to travel' (Davies, 2011).

The academic impact of displacement is now starting to be robustly researched. A major source of data about the impact of IDP identity on learning outcomes derives from a 2010 UNICEF report on students' competency levels in Northern and Eastern Provinces. The report documents the delivery, scoring and processing of a set of tests of Tamil and mathematics used to place displaced and returned learners in the Accelerated Learning Programmes (ALP). A reference group of non-displaced learners was used for comparison. The results showed a sharp disparity in achievement between the reference group schools and the schools in the Eastern province selected for inclusion in the ALP – albeit with a considerable disparity *within* the schools in this group. In the Northern province the pattern was more mixed, but there was a significant achievement deficit associated with any form of displacement – about three years learning for those still in IDP camps or in schools which had restarted, and about one and a half years for those who had been displaced but found places in schools which had continued to function normally. The impact of displacement was also greatest among younger learners. Those in restarted schools achieved at a level of about 0.9 below the reference group mean. The three-grade difference had implications for their progress in an ALP programme – a typical displaced person in a regular school may need to spend a year in the ALP, while a typical learner who is still displaced or is in a newly restarted school may need about two years. The deficit in Tamil language is much larger in primary than in secondary grade – indicating 'emergency action'. The achievement deficit among displaced learners in regular schools almost disappears by secondary stage, but not in restarted schools.

The report points up the difficulty of rigorous research on the performance of IDP children. The exact numbers and locations of learners to be tested were difficult to determine. Schools had been closed or damaged, and some students were not attending school at all. The reference group was not intended to reflect the national standard of achievement, as the provinces were the lowest achieving anyway; instead they reflected the typical performance of Tamil medium students who were deemed not to have suffered significant ill effects from the conflict. Yet in spite of the difficulties in the research, it is an important and unique study which shows how IDP status impacts on specific learning areas and then, by implication, how something like a three year gap in achievement will continue into opportunities in the future. It also provides specific pointers for action in terms of the type and length of catch-up programmes needed.

Strategy

This leads on to consideration of strategies that are being used to try to close gaps and enhance provision. For humanitarian work, the agencies take different responsibilities for sectors, and UNICEF is the sector lead for education, doing much work in providing temporary learning spaces (TLSs). UNICEF and GIZ support the training of psychosocial support in the Northern province; there are also Training of Trainers programmes for inexperienced primary-level teachers, with training in basic classroom pedagogy, the goals of the national curriculum and the Child-Friendly Schools concept. GTZ (now GIZ) reported to the author in 2010 of their work with 'disadvantaged' children and young people in the post-conflict and poverty areas of Trincomalee. This included beneficiaries of students in welfare camps (835) and students in rehabilitation camps (199) who were doing GCE O level.

One important part of inter-agency working is forming clusters for advocacy work. One of the problems was that education was not seen as a priority for humanitarian aid. After extensive advocacy work, humanitarian agencies were persuaded to create an education cluster, and in 2009 there were 34 countries who had done this, including Sri Lanka. After the large-scale displacement, the education cluster in Sri Lanka helped ensure that early childhood education and development (ECED) was provided in IDP camps, and facilitated the distribution of educational materials (Papadopolous, 2010).

As a result of advocacy by the education cluster to consider education as a right to which all children should be entitled despite their circumstances, the Sri Lankan army had made it a priority by May 2009 to secure spaces for schools within the new camps. In Jaffna, cluster advocacy and negotiation enabled many IDP students to attend schools outside the camps and others were able to join classes in host schools, thus promoting a sense of normality and gradual healing in the aftermath of the protracted conflict (UNICEF, 2010).

During the height of the IDP influx into camps, the Ministry of Education, in collaboration with UNICEF, supported the administration of a rapid assessment of IDP children in two districts. The assessment indicated that many children were at or below the minimum learning competency for their age group and would require a special programme to help them catch up – the Accelerated Learning Programme, now discussed more fully.

An Accelerated Learning Programme (ALP) is a widely used catch-up strategy, as in other countries who have undergone conflict (Davies 2012 forthcoming). In these provinces of Sri Lanka, this is designed to be a temporary school-based intervention to help students rapidly reach their age-appropriate learning competency, thus promoting Grade 3–9 retention. The design of the ALP ensures that older students will be able to sit Ordinary level and Advanced level exams with minimum disruption (UNICEF, 2009)[5]. But placement and organization are not simple. UNICEF explain how the reported proportion of IDPs in still-functioning schools tends to be quite low, so it may not be viable to put together ALP classes in such schools, and in some cases the most appropriate response may be to identify IDP learners in need of special attention and offer them remedial classes either during or after school hours. In restarted schools, there may be a need for two or three 'tracks' – regular (learners in age-appropriate classes), ALP plus 1 and ALP plus 2. But the viability will depend on the number of learners in each grade. There is also the problem of learners returning during the school year, although this may be less of a problem in 2011 than it was in 2010. In IDP camps, the basic situation is similar, but there is a real question of whether any provision at all is viable within the camp, since the inhabitants are in the process of being resettled[6].

Vocational Training is another initiative which targets IDP youth. In OCHA categories, this comes under 'Early Recovery' rather than education.

Vocational education in a range of occupational fields is currently being provided across the Northern province with the support of the Vocational Training Authority and various international partner organizations. In Vavuniya district, the Government Agent office has specifically requested agencies to provide appropriate training to resettled youth for employment in factories to be established shortly in the area. Yet as Williams (2010) points out, plans for the expansion of vocational training have not been prioritized in government spending plans.

Surrounding the practical initiatives on catch-up and employment preparation, there are nonetheless continuing debates about return and reconciliation. Badurdeen (2010) makes the point that younger generations of the northern Tamils have no memories or experiences of the formerly multi-ethnic northern communities where Tamils and Muslims co-existed peacefully for hundreds of years. She cites the view that there should be attempts to revive such memories and undertake initiatives to promote the renewal of relationships between Tamils and Muslims.

But cultural reintegration will relate also to basic provision for living. The most recent report at the time of writing is that Menik Farm is to close. The previous year, 5000 inmates were ordered to move at 24 hours notice, when students were in the middle of their A level exams (BBC Tamil Service, 2010). Now the remaining 7,400 people (2097 families) will be relocated. This will be to a new village called Kombavil, in a remote area. While the government says that they will have good facilities, Tamil politicians point out that they will have to go to areas which are little more than newly-cleared jungle. Their old villages are designated by the government as 'special economic development areas' or on land the military wants to keep. As well as concerns about the substandard housing they will receive, fears have been expressed that there appear to be no facilities for schools, places of worship or even water (Groundviews, 2011). Strategy and advocacy by international agencies has to take account of a constantly shifting political and economic dynamic with regard to IDPs which surrounds any educational initiative.

Critical Discussion and Theoretical Insights

The accounts above of IDPs and education in Sri Lanka generate important underlying theoretical issues which have implications for future strategy.

Three concerns discussed here are the question of what constitutes a 'host'; the political economy questions of class and gender; and the relation of IDP strategy to peacebuilding in the future.

Brun (2010) undertakes a more theoretical analysis of the categories of 'IDPs' and 'hosts', using the Puttalam experience. This raises policy questions as well as social questions. UN type advocacy is for a separate category of IDPs, in need of specific assistance. The International Committee of the Red Cross (ICRC) on the other hand is critical of working with internal displacement as a separate humanitarian category, instead giving priority to those with the most urgent needs. Brun discusses how forced migration represents a 'throwntogetherness' in Massey's (2005) term. She also mentions the welcome by both Muslim and Sinhalese residents which was referred to earlier. Yet there are two notions of 'hospitality', conditional and unconditional. The welcome initially may have been unconditional, and for Muslims linked to the Islamic obligation or ethic around hospitality. This did ease the phase of reception. Yet as humanitarian agencies moved in, the hosts felt somewhat sidelined and their response became more conditional. The arrival of northern Muslims also altered the existing balance between Muslims, Sinhalese and Tamils. Responsibility then becomes an institutional one, of who would decide who is to be welcomed. This would have particular implications for the placing of IDP children in schools and who bears the costs. A key question was competing for local resources, not just in health but, as we saw, university quotas, which did not increase to take account of new arrivals. Sovereignty over place is challenged. 'The arrival of the Muslims was a symbol of the war coming closer: could they trust people who had lived with the war, what kind of violence did they bring with them?' (Brun, 2010: 9). Northern Muslims would proudly announce their Tamil language as the pure Tamil in contrast to the Puttalam Muslims' Tamil. There have been violent encounters between northern and local Muslims. Yet once settled, for many Muslims, returning to the north is like being displaced again.

As Brun points out, the concept of 'hosts' as a category has received limited attention in forced migration studies and is taken for granted as a category that comes into existence when IDPs or refugees arrive. They are presented as a single category summarized as 'host communities', 'the local people' or 'the surrounding population'. Their own heterogeneity is not addressed. 'Old' IDPs in places such as Jaffna often host 'new' IDPs, which renders them even more vulnerable because they do not receive assistance (IDMC, 2011a). IDPs may on the other hand influence the host in beneficial ways (as we saw with IDPs having higher levels of female education).

Implications for strategy around education would be not just to acknowledge the needs of host communities but to engage in more complex analysis of that host environment to determine the existing opportunities within their educational landscape which new arrivals will of necessity interrupt. This links to a second analytic demand which is the use of a political economy approach around disparities in power, socio-economic level and gender. While GoSL may prefer to construct the conflict as an ethnic one, about disharmony between 'races', the Strategic Conflict Assessments show the reality as one of a struggle for power and resources and a history of discrimination. The military 'victory' has not addressed the causes of the conflict, and the perception of continuing – or even increased – disparities for those groups forced to displace and then suffer disadvantage on return means perpetuation of grievance. Hellmann-Rajanayagam (2010) reports education having a high priority in the North and East during the LTTE administration, even if that educational achievement did not always translate into professional mobility and success. Educational deprivation during the last phase of the war, in the camps and even now, is again perceived as a sign and symptom of deliberate discrimination against the Tamils by the Sinhalese, whether this is the case or not.

The dilemma for international and local agencies is how far to bring such issues to the surface. A visit by the author to a peace festival taking place in a school in 2010 revealed an IDP school right next door for children from the nearby camp, but whose pupils were not invited. The reason was held to be insufficient drinks and snacks. The emphasis in the social cohesion activity was on cultural dancing and listening to prayers of 'other' religions, with no mention of issues of conflict, politics or displacement. This appears to condone the official line constructing the problem as one of inter-ethnic 'tolerance'; yet for agencies to be critical of government policy and action risks their operations being swiftly curtailed by GoSL. The trick appears to be to focus on supporting those whose rights may be denied but not using the language of rights, rather of 'disadvantaged groups', 'psychosocial care' and 'remedial education', which is not threatening.

As has been seen during this chapter, gender differentials are also part of IDP experience. Ironically, traditional gender roles are sometimes loosened in the camps, with women having to take on new economic responsibilities or challenge sexual violence from men around them. But as Bandarage (2010) points out, such relative loosening of traditional gender roles has rarely been accompanied by new opportunities or women's long-term empowerment. As elsewhere, the feminization of poverty has been deepened by armed conflict and violence. Bandarage argues for peace education through 'creative modalities' (without specifying what those are). She wants re-education and reintegration of remaining LTTE women cadres, especially members of the former suicide bomber unit, into civilian society. But for her, this and other integration requires '*transformation of the structures of militarism and male dominance as well as the hierarchies of class, ethnicity and caste at the local, regional and international levels*' (2010: 665). This is a somewhat ambitious demand; but certainly a challenge to militarism and patriarchy could be a valuable component of education, if permitted.

This leads to the third complex question, of the link between IDP education and peacebuilding. Humanitarian assistance to IDPs does not normally have an explicit peace-building objective. Chapman et al. (2009), in a major evaluation of donor-supported activities in conflict-sensitive development in Sri Lanka, reported that when peace and conflict assessments were conducted they were found to be 'static'. Some but not all mentioned 'do no harm' but none expounded explicit theories of change. Implicitly, the expectation would be to further the peace process through providing economic gains, through resettlement and thereby improved livelihoods. It is significant that the US Embassy (2009) reported that aid was going to physical reconstruction or rehabilitation 'to help conflict-affected communities return to normality as quickly as possible'. There seemed no analysis of what 'normality' in these areas had been and the problems that this normality had caused. Nor was there mention of IDPs.

Yet while IDPs are not subject to international law, there has been a growing trend within the international community to incorporate the return of IDPs within peace processes. Price (2010) in a discussion of return and recovery in Sri Lanka distinguishes between negative and positive peace. For those trapped in camps or trying to return, the benefits of peace remain to be seen. In the final months of the war, many IDPs faced brutal exposure to the conflict, being used as human shields by the LTTE and as victims of indiscriminate shelling by the Sri Lankan Army. Limited access to humanitarian agencies led to a number of compromises in humanitarian standards. Although the fighting has stopped, the government is continuing to treat all IDPs as potential security threats. Price argues for a new approach to resolving displacement, a new 'social contract' between the government and the displaced. She does not mention education, but the provision of quality schooling would presumably be part of this contract, and be a constituent of positive peace.

The question is whether in tackling displacement the government would indeed seize the opportunity for the 'social and economic change' that Price demands. The analysis of this chapter is that conflict and displacement have created a predominantly highly negative educational situation for those affected, and that education itself is currently located within, at best, a similarly 'negative peace'. For any future positive peace, the overall return and recovery process would need to be one trusted by the Tamils as a genuine effort to ensure land and livelihoods, as well as educational opportunities. Further, as this chapter has shown, the voices of the displaced about education (as well as the voices of their 'hosts') have to be heard clearly in any humanitarian or peace building work.

Questions for Further Discussion

Should IDPs form a special category for humanitarian assistance, or should priority simply be given to those in need of specific assistance (which may include 'hosts')?

How far should aid agencies and NGOs insist on a political analysis of the causes and impacts of conflict in their work and negotiations, and how far should they seem to remain neutral?

Should IDP interventions be linked to peacekeeping and peacebuilding?

Notes

1 Liberation Tigers of Tamil Eelam.
2 The rights are detailed in the *Guiding Principles on International Displacement*, Internal Displacement Monitoring Centre (IDMC) www.internal-displacement.org/guidingprinciples.
3 An NGO: Facilitating Local Initiatives for Conflict Transformation. The initials now stand for FaciLitating Initiatives for social Cohesion and Transformation, to reflect the government's stance that the conflict is over.
4 By the author as part of a GIZ review team.
5 These are slightly different from 'Open Schools' programmes in the plantation areas of Sri Lanka, which are not part of normal school programmes, but specifically designed for out-of-school young people and drop-outs, and which deliberately do not recreate 'normal' school activities and authoritarian teacher-student relationships, Davies 2011.

6 A recent report stated that Menik Farm camp was to close 'within weeks' BBC (2011).

References

Badurdeen F. (2010), *Ending Internal Displacement: the long-term IDPs in Sri Lanka,* Working Paper Series no 66. Oxford: Refugee Studies Centre

Bandarage, A. (2010), 'Women, Armed Conflict and Peacemaking in Sri Lanka: Toward a Political Economy Perspective', *Asian Politics and Policy* 2,4, 653–67.

BBC News South Asia (2011), 'Sri Lanka's Menik Farm Refugee Camp "to close"'. www.bbc.co.uk/news/world-south-asia-15007375. (Accessed November 2011).

BBC Tamil Service (2010), 'IDPs Ordered to Move'. www.bbc.co.uk/sinhala/news/story/2010/08/100817_menik_farm.shtml. (Accessed November 2011).

Brun, C. (2010), 'Hospitality: becoming "IDPs" and "hosts" in protracted displacement' *Journal of Refugee Studies* login.westlaw.co.uk/maf/wluk/app/document?src=toce&&docguidep1395 202DO16 (Accessed 12 September 2011).

Chapman, N., Duncan, D., Timberman, D. and Abeygunawardena, K. (2009), *Evaluation of Donor-Supported Activities in Conflict-sensitive Development and Conflict Prevention and Peace Building in Sri Lanka,* Paris: Report for OECD.

Cohen, R. (2008), *Listening to the Voices of the Displaced: Lessons Learned,* Brookings-Bern Project on Internal Displacement, September 2008, Washington, DC.

Davies, L. (2011), *Promoting Education in Countries affected by Fragility and Conflict: Sri Lanka Case Study.* Commissioned paper for GIZ, Frankfurt.

De Silva, N. and Punchihewa, A. (2010), *Protecting Children on the Move: A Study based in the Probation District of Hambantota, Sri Lanka,* Sri Lanka: Save The Children.

Ferris, E. and Winthrop, R. (2010), *Education and Displacement: Assessing Conditions for Refugees and Internally Displaced Persons affected by Conflict,* Background Paper for the EFA Global Monitoring Report. unesdoc.unesco.org/images/0019/001907/190715e.pdf (Accessed 12 October 2011).

FLICT (2006), *FLICT: Concept and structure,* Colombo: Facilitating Local Initiatives for Conflict Transformation.

Fonseka, B. and Cassiere-Daniel, M. (2009), *Home away from Home: Children, Displacement and Protection in Sri Lanka.* Sri Lanka: Save the Children.

Groundviews (October, 2011), *Re-displacement of Menik Farm Inmates to Kombavil (Mullativu),* groundviews.org/2011/10/03/re-displacement-of-menik-farm-inmates-to-kombavil-mullativu. . (Accessed January 2012).

—(January, 2008), *The Divide Between Muslims and Tamils: Perspectives of an IDP* groundviews. org/2008/01/16/the-divide-between-muslims-and-tamils-perspective-of-an-idp/. (Accessed January 2012).

Haniffa, F. (2011), 'The Citizens' Commission on the Expulsion of the Muslims from the Northern Province by the LTTE in October 1990'. *Groundviews* 21.Nov 2011, groundviews.org/2011/11/21/

the-citizens%e2%80%99-commission-on-the-expulsion-of-the-muslims-from-the-northern-province-by-the-ltte-in-october-1990/. (Accessed November 2011).

Hellman-Rayamayagam, D. (2010), *Desk Study with recommendations for independent evaluation: Education for Social Cohesion in Sri Lanka*. GTZ Internal paper.

Hurwit, C. (2011), 'IDP Education lacking in Sri Lanka', *The Bowdoin Orient,* Vol CXL, No 1 orient. bowdoin.edu/orient/article/php?date=2011-01-21§ion+2&id=4 (Accessed 9 September 2011).

Husein, F. et al, (2011), 'Prevalence of War-related Mental Health Conditions and Association with Displacement Status in Postwar Jaffna District, Sri Lanka', *Journal of the American Medical Association* Vol 306 No 5, 522–31.

IDMC (2011a), *Sri Lanka: IDPs and returnees remain in need of protection and assistance.* Internal Displacement Monitoring Centre, Norwegian Refugee Council, Switzerland: Geneva.

—(2011b), *Property, Livelihood, Education and Other Economic, Social and Cultural Rights,* Internal Displacement Monitoring Centre, Norwegian Refugee Council, Switzerland: Geneva.

Irin News (2011), 'Sri Lanka: could do better in the East', www.irinnews.org/photo/Details.aspx?Im ageId=201111030940270829. (Accessed November 2011).

Massey. D. (2005), *For Space,* London: Sage.

OCHA (2010), *Joint Humanitarian Update: North and East Sri Lanka* Report No 29 October – November 2010.

—(2011), *Sri Lanka Report,* 2 November Sri Lanka: OCHA.

O'Malley, B. (2010), *Education Under Attack,* Paris: UNESCO.

Papadopolous, N. (2010), *Achievements and challenges of the Education Cluster in the occupied Palestinian territory, Somalia and Sri Lanka.* Background paper for the UNESCP 2011 EFA Monitoring report. unesdoc.unesco.org/images/0019/001907/190776e.pdf (Accessed 12 September 2011).

Price, N. (2010), 'Integrating "Return" with "Recovery": Utilising the Return Process in the Transition to Positive Peace: A Case Study of Sri Lanka', *The Round Table* Vol 99, No 410, 529–45.

Shankar, J. (2011), *Post-Conflict Reconstruction in Sri Lanka and Cyprus: Avoiding a Stalemate,* Senior Thesis, Claremont McKenna College.

Tamil Week (2011), *Report from Peace Women.* www. peacewoman.org/news (Accessed 12 December 2011).

UNESCO (2011), *EFA Global Monitoring Report* Paris: UNESCO.

UNICEF (2010), *An assessment of students' competency levels in Grades 3–9 in Northern and Eastern Provinces,* Sri Lanka: UNICEF.

Save The Children (2009), *Case Study: Robeka – Sri Lanka.* London: Save The Children.

Sunday Times (2011), 'Northern Education in major Gridlock' *Sri Lanka Sunday Times,* Sunday 11 September. sundaytimes.lk/110911/Newsnws__012.html (Accessed 12 September 2011).

Williams, J. (2010), *The Impact of Conflict and Displacement (2006–2010) on Education in Sri Lanka,* Background paper for the UNESCO EFA Monitoring Report.

UN SRCAC (2011), *UN Office of the Special Representative for Children and Armed Conflict Report,* 23 April 2011. www.un.org/children/conflict/english/srilanka.html. (Accessed November 2011).

US Embassy (2009), 'US Ambassador opens two schools rehabilitated by the US Government in Trincomalee District', *Press Release* 10 November 2009, Colombo.

7 Returnees and the Challenges for Education Reform in Bosnia and Herzegovina

Marina Bowder and Valery Perry

Chapter Outline

Abstract

The three- and -a-half year war in Bosnia and Herzegovina resulted in the displacement of approximately half the country's population of 4 million, including both internally displaced persons and refugees. Since the signing of the Dayton Peace Agreement in late 1995, there have been efforts to support return and, in particular, minority return (the return of people to a community where they would now be in a demographic minority). However, with some exceptions, the wartime ethnic cleansing operations were successful in creating much more homogenous communities throughout the country. In those communities where there *is* diversity, however, the education structure makes reintegration and inclusion extremely difficult, as the country's education structure and curricula are defined by ethno-national, rather than civic, practices and values. This practice has a particular effect on minority returnees and their re-integration into a community; an effect that ultimately could render lasting, sustainable return a failure. This chapter reviews the education challenges in Bosnia and Herzegovina, with a focus on the efforts to address the divisive nature of curricular content which, if unchanged, will cement fear and distrust among new generations of citizens and leaders, and prevent the country's long-term democratic consolidation.

Introduction

'A democracy is more than a form of government; it is primarily a mode of associated living, of conjoint communicated experience' (Dewey, 1916: 87).

The education system in post-war Bosnia and Herzegovina (BiH) has been criticized for being, if not a cause, then a symptom, reflection and enhancer of the ethno-national political divisions that continue to serve as a source for instability and insecurity. With rare exceptions, every school in BiH has its own 'ethnic flavor' ensuring that one of the country's three constituent peoples is dominant – schools reflect the aspirations and educational goals of that group to a greater or lesser extent, leaving any other students (returnees, minorities, others) either to fit in and quietly assimilate, or, ultimately, to find another school where 'their' people will be in charge. The impact of such a social experiment is worrisome, and at this point an entire generation of young people have now been born and educated in systems designed during the war and its aftermath.

In the general elections held in October 2010, the group of first-time voters born in or around 1992 had the opportunity to cast their ballots within an electoral system that is in many ways just as fragmented as their country's schools, textbooks and curricula. (Further reflecting this fragmentation, as of November 2011, over a year after the elections, the political parties had still failed to form a state-level government.) At a time when the country still seems to be in crisis, the questions of what children learn in schools; whether the education system serves as a tool for reintegration of returning displaced persons – or the reverse – and whether schools prepare them for life in a heterogeneous country that aspires to membership in a very diverse European Union (EU); are critical.

This chapter will focus on the challenges that the country's educators, and in particular education reformers, face in the light of the wartime population transfers and the resultant difficulties in (re)integrating refugees and displaced persons. First, a short review of the wartime displacement and post-war efforts in support of return is provided. This is followed by an overview of the challenges of the divided country's post-war education systems, and a brief summary of efforts (overwhelmingly driven by international actors) to reform the divisive wartime systems. Next, key features of the divisive curricular content of the country's multiple curricula and textbooks are detailed; an element often overlooked as more immediately visible issues such as 'two schools under one roof' receive international attention, yet which is at the core of both the problem and possible solutions: what and how children learn. The extent to which the 'us vs. them' narrative permeates curricular materials is of particular consequence for minority returnee families seeking to re-integrate into their pre-war communities. The chapter closes with concluding reflections on the technical, pedagogical and political prospects for reform.

A number of questions will weave their way through this discussion, more as food for thought than as a quest for definitive answers. In a country still suffering from an identity crisis of sorts, how can content – including course modules, teaching materials and didactic approaches – make a dent in a system that is otherwise structured around a framework emphasizing the predominance of one group? Can school-level grassroots efforts make a contribution to the broader macro-level, systemic discussions and debates regarding the nature and flavor of BiH as a democratic state? If schools are not accessible to and appropriate for all young citizens, including minorities and returnees, can return in BiH even be considered sustainable? Finally, can schools play a role in ultimately consolidating the goals of peace by cultivating a future electorate comfortable with the benefits, compromises, challenges and strengths of a heterogeneous country forged by war but united by a shared vision of integration into Euro-Atlantic structures?

BiH's Wartime Displacement and the Political Consequences

Today's Bosnia and Herzegovina was created in the aftermath of the wars of Yugoslav succession that devastated the region in the 1990s. Following a brief conflict in Slovenia in 1991 and a longer war in Croatia, war in BiH raged for three and a half years, Generally speaking, the war was fought among the Bosniaks (Muslims), the Bosnian Croats (Catholics) and Bosnian Serbs (Orthodox Christians), though many persons of mixed or undeclared background were affected by the violence as political and military leaders alternately fought for an independent BiH, the creation of 'ethnically pure' mini-states or annexation to neighboring Croatia or rump-Yugoslavia (Serbia and Montenegro). Significant population transfers – especially in the first year of the war – reduced a formerly highly heterogeneous and diverse population map into a place where territory and ethnically 'clean' populations dominated. Serb forces, with support from the former Yugoslav military (the JNA) and Serbian paramilitaries, made quick progress in the first months of the war. It is estimated that 100,000 people were killed in the fighting, and half the population of approximately four million displaced from their homes. The displacement was complete, as persons pushed out of their homes either at gunpoint, or by pressure or pre-emptive fear-driven choice, fled to other parts of the country or abroad. Ethnic cleansing operations in the Drina valley in eastern Bosnia which marked the start of the war changed the nature of the populations of Zvornik, Visegrad, Foca and other towns, as Bosniak populations were expelled or killed. Doboj and Brcko followed, together mapping a new geographic construct called 'Republika Srpska'. In others parts of the country, the 'war within a war' between the Croats and the Bosniaks had a similarly deleterious demographic impact. Towns in central Bosnia including Jajce, Jablanica and Kiseljak experienced refugee flows and abandoned villages. Towards the end of the war in 1995, the 're-taking' of some territories by the Army of BiH led to further displacement, often of the already displaced.[1] Rural and urban populations shifted with significant consequences for the cultural and demographic life of cities, most notably in Sarajevo (Stefansson, 2008).

Internationally brokered peace talks led the warring parties (including the then Presidents of neighboring Croatia and Serbia) to sign a peace deal in late 1995 (the General Framework Agreement for Peace, or Dayton Accords) (Burg and Shoup, 2000; Bose, 2002). The Dayton Agreement included an Annex that aimed to enshrine the right of return. Annex 7 sought to ensure that citizens who had been displaced could not only have the option to return to their pre-war home, but would be encouraged to do so as the country sought to rebuild. Point 1 of Article 1 in Annex 7 specifically links return to lasting peace: 'The early return of refugees and displaced persons is an important objective of the settlement of the conflict in Bosnia and Herzegovina.' This could be seen as an idealistic attempt to reconstruct the diversity of the country after the violence; or as a cynical attempt to reverse the damages that was caused by local warlords, and which international observers failed to prevent. However, as a component of the peace agreement, it committed the parties to implementation. The United Nations High Commissioner for Refugees (UNHCR) was in particular noted in Article I: 'The Parties call upon the United Nations High Commissioner for Refugees ('UNHCR') to develop in close consultation with asylum countries and the Parties a repatriation plan that will allow for an early, peaceful, orderly and phased return of refugees and displaced persons, which may include priorities for certain areas and certain categories of refugees. The Parties agree to implement such a plan and to confirm their international agreements and internal laws to it.[2] The International Committee of the Red Cross and the United Nations Development Program were also specifically noted, together with a broad statement noting the possible involvement of other NGOs and international organizations in the many different aspects of return (temporary and permanent housing, reintegration assistance, etc.

The highest number of returns occurred in the two years following the end of the war, primarily consisting of 'majority returns'. In the first years after the war, minority return was slow, hampered by a sense of insecurity among potential returnees, direct attacks on returnee communities, and the significantly destroyed housing stock (Mooney, 2008). Domestic leaders, particularly in the RS but elsewhere as well, made virtually no steps to welcome back the displaced. Pressures for refugees to return from countries such as Germany increased the need for workable return solutions, though 'minority return' (the return of people to a community where they would now be in a minority; for example, a Bosniak or Croat in Banja Luka in the Republika Srpska, a Croat in a Bosniak-majority municipality or canton such as Sarajevo, in the Federation, or a Serb in Mostar, in the Federation) remained elusive. The domestic Commission for Real Property Claims of Refugees and Displaced Persons established by the peace agreement faced a combination of technical challenges, but even more, confronted a lack of political will by leaders to allow the Commission truly to facilitate minority return. The international community, initially reluctant to engage too heavily in the civilian aspects of the Accords (hoping for a quick 'in and out' intervention) soon became more involved, viewing implementation of the agreement as critical not only in re-building the country but also in ending the international engagement. In 1999, a significant program called PLIP (the Property Law Implementation Plan) began the complex logistical process of ensuring that people who owned property had formal claim to that property, and could in turn either choose to return physically, or to at least sell their property as they made their new life elsewhere (Phuong, 2000; Jansen, 2008). Mooney attributes the progress in minority return from 2000–2 to four factors: freedom of movement, security, property repossession and reconstruction (Mooney, 2008).

While progress was certainly made, the question remains: was return – and in particular, minority return – successful? The country has not had a census since before the war, but a number of conclusions can be drawn. First, the *property* return process was by and large successful, with over 95% of claims fulfilled. This success rate, however, does not mirror the actual rate of individuals and families reclaiming their property and staying in their pre-war home. Many opted to sell their property, often to other displaced persons, and re-make their lives elsewhere in the face of challenges including blatant discrimination, lack of economic opportunities, and access to public services and support structures, including unbiased education (Mooney, 2008). However, Toal and Dahlman (2011: 296) point out a number of pockets of success, noting urban municipalities in Sarajevo, Banja Luka, Brcko, Prijedor, Bijeljina, Zvornik and Doboj experiencing somewhat more significant numbers of returnees. They further analyze available data to conclude that it is simplistic to claim return was either a roaring success or an abject failure:

> 'The charge that the implementation of Annex 7 has failed is, in the end, more an argument about the greater endurance of the legacy of ethnic cleansing than a fair evaluation of its implementation. The sustained effort by international agencies and local non-governmental organizations succeeded in helping thousands of ordinary Bosnians better their lives and achieve a modicum of justice after a brutal war.... Yet the low level of sustained minority returns and the relative success of soft obstructionism and land allocation strategy as tactics designed to consolidate the demographic "achievement" of ethnic cleansing raise a different possibility: Annex 7 may well have succeeded while, at the same time, so also has ethnic-cleansing' (Toal and Dahlman, 2011: 305).

The post-Dayton BiH within which real or property return was happening was (and remains) a complex, gerrymandered construction whose map reflected the front lines and minefields of the war. BiH's governing structure and internal boundaries were formalized in the peace accords, and based on political imperatives and the effects of ethnic cleansing rather than administrative logic, consisting of a convoluted geographic patchwork of state, entity, cantonal and municipal levels of government crafted to appease the varying national factions. The state of BiH created at Dayton was intentionally weak, with power-sharing guarantees, including minimum representation, ethnic quotas and national veto options for the three constituent peoples embedded throughout. BiH consists of two highly autonomous entities which have held the real decision-making and operational power. The Federation of Bosnia and Herzegovina (FBiH), often referred to as the 'Muslim-Croat Federation', was initially created during the war in 1994, and comprises 51% of the territory of BiH. The Republika Srpska (RS), also a political construct forged in the war, makes up 49% of the territory of BiH. The entities are structured very differently, with the RS highly centralized and the FBiH highly decentralized, with powers devolved to ten cantons. Five of these cantons have large Bosniak majorities,[3] three have large Croat majorities,[4] and two are very mixed.[5] In addition BiH has 143 municipalities, and one special administrative district in Brčko (in north-east BiH), which is held in condominium by *both* entities, but is in fact controlled by neither. This convoluted constitutional and political arrangement might better be called a compromise than a structure.[6] It reflects the serious political obstacles to reform and reconciliation in the country, and the environment in which reintegration and reconciliation efforts must proceed.

These obstacles have seemed increasingly dire since a renewed political stalemate took hold of the country in 2006. After some years of limited progress in terms of state-strengthening and post-war reform, BiH's already shaky foundation began to be compromised through a spiraling and reinforcing domestic political conflict that once again brought to the fore the existential questions of BiH's territory, power and powersharing. A constitutional reform proposal (the 'April package'), was rejected by Haris Silajdzic's party ('Party for Bosnia and Herzegovina') in the spring of 2006, relegating to history reforms that were much more robust in terms of state-strengthening elements than anything seen since. The autumn 2006 general elections saw Milorad Dodik elected as Prime Minister of the RS, benefiting from Silajdzic's constitutional gamble and intransigence and in turn positioning himself as the defender of the RS. These developments occurred against the backdrop of an increasingly divided community, as a debate unfolded on whether and how quickly the Office of the High Representative (OHR) could be closed. Montenegro's independence referendum in 2006, and Kosovo's unilateral declaration of independence (UDI) in 2008, reinforced by an International Court of Justice ruling in 2010 that did not find the UDI to be against international law, increased concerns about threats of secession by the RS. Post-2006 constitutional reform initiatives resulted in little, and in late 2011 even minimal constitutional reforms required by the European Court of Human Rights have eluded success, perhaps even undercutting popular confidence in such efforts due to their lack of results and the visible hardening of party lines in the process. In 2011 there have been several subsequent 'crises' that illustrate both the weakness of the state and the inability of international pressure or incentive (such as promises of EU membership) to remedy the problems (McMahon and Western, 2009; Chivvis, 2010, Bassuener and Weber 2010). Against the background of this elite-level stalemate, at the most grassroots level of the country's schools, the political divisions of the country are playing out in equally concerning ways.

Education in Post-Dayton Bosnia and Herzegovina

The current fragmented nature of the education system in BiH reflects both the schools established during the three and a half years of war and the post-war constitutional structure that resulted in a state consisting of two entities, three peoples and a seemingly endless number of consequential power-sharing problems. There are no state level competences in education (only a coordinating role lacking in any real power whatsoever); there is no state-level Ministry of Education (MoE), no state-level strategy for improving education, and no single phone number for either education experts or Brussels-based donors to call to modernize and reform the country's education system. Instead, each of BiH's two entities has an MoE, and while the MoE in the Republika Srpska (RS) manages a very centralized education system in that entity, the highly *decentralized* Federation is further dissected into ten cantonal MoEs. Those cantons implement either a mildly pro-Bosniak or emphatically pro-Croat curriculum (see below) and have varying levels of formal and informal coordination. The District of Brcko has its own Education Department as well (see Perry 2006; OSCE Mission to BiH 2007a).

The state-level Ministry of Civil Affairs (MoCA) has an education portfolio which has a limited scope of work; a state-level Education Agency has been developed and technically has an advisory capacity but is still struggling to function in any meaningful way; and all of the country's Ministers of Education are supposed to meet periodically under the auspices of the Conference of Ministers of Education, chaired by MoCA, which can advise and consult on matters but cannot (or will not) set standards or make policy decisions that would be applicable and/or required for all lower-level bodies. (As of November 2011, the Conference has failed to meet for well over a year.) No state level body has any enforcement mechanism to ensure that standards are enforced.

Curricula are similarly fragmented, with the end result being that there are distinct Bosniak, Croat and Serb curricula. With the exception of schools in Brcko, any given school has a dominant ethnic 'flavor' based on the location and the majority constituent people in that location – a school will implement one of the three curricula, and will likely have a name, symbols and commemorative days in line with the majority group within. Over 50 'two schools under one roof' exist in the Federation where the population is sufficiently mixed to result in schools sharing a building and implementing both a Bosniak and Croat curriculum for the respective students in different wings, floors or shifts. In the RS, in the limited number of areas that have experienced sufficient minority returns, non-Serb students (primarily Bosniaks) study the emphatically pro-Serb RS curriculum, but occasionally have the opportunity to study 'their' national group of subjects (in 'their' own language), including history, geography, language and religion.[7] Brcko is the only part of BiH where students study according to a single Brcko District curriculum, and schools are completely integrated; however, even in these schools (among the most reformed in the country) students may opt to use one of three sets of textbooks (one for each language) and may study some of the 'national' subjects partly separated from one another (see Perry 2006; OSCE Mission to BiH 2007a).

A UNESCO report examining the impact of war and divisive politics expresses the impact of such policies quite clearly: 'Values inculcated in school can make children less susceptible to the kind of prejudice, bigotry, extreme nationalism, racism and lack of tolerance that can lead to violent conflict. When the discrimination and power relationships that maintain social, political and economic exclusion find expression in the classroom, however, education can have the opposite effect. Schools can act as conduits for transmitting attitudes, ideas and beliefs that make societies more prone to violence' (2011: 167). This assessment is even more important when considering cases of societies torn apart by violent conflict, and struggling to build a just peace in a divided political environment. In the divisive environment of BiH, the role of schools and formal education in promoting tolerance and respect for diversity – let alone facilitating the reintegration of returnee students – seemed dim.

Education Reform Efforts

Until the late years of the twentieth century, education has for all practical purposes been a domestic issue, though the prominence of education as an important human rights issue – particularly in divided and conflict-affected societies – has grown.[8] The need for education reform in BiH was evident even as the war raged on, and numerous assessments were prepared years before the international community increased its interest in the issue (see Perry, 2003: 45). In the years following the war, there were many different efforts aimed at improving the education system in BiH from a technical standpoint by organizations including UNICEF, UNESCO, EC-Technical Assistance to Education Reform (EC-TAER), the World Bank and others. The OSCE Mission to Bosnia and Herzegovina (MBiH) addressed some aspects of education within its human rights portfolio, and the Office of the High Representative (OHR)[9] had a small team also addressing the issue within the context of human rights and return. In fact it was the issue of return that pushed education up the priority list for many organizations, as it became clear that promotion of return (and particularly minority return) would fail if returnees could not send their children to schools in a given community, either for mobility reasons or safety concerns, blatant obstruction or valid concerns about the content being taught by the now-dominant majority that 'owned' the school. The impact of war and displacement on education has been increasingly acknowledged. The 2011 Education for All Global Monitoring report, *The Hidden Crisis: Armed Conflict and Education*, notes that 'forced displacement is a direct threat to education, both for people categorized as refugees and for IDPs', thoroughly documenting the problems of educational access during war and the subsequent often fragile peace (2011: 19).

This was certainly true in BiH. As early as 1997, extracts from newly written textbooks began filtering into the press: would-be-returnees thus gained startling views of the material their children would be expected to study were they to enroll at the local school, and education content moved to the top of priority concerns for families with children. This added to already existing concerns about security – concerns that were inevitably increased by the incidents that did occur, most notably where returnees were in sufficient numbers to be seen as a threat by the now-majority population. One egregious example of such 'non-welcoming' practices is the barrier of furniture erected by the management of Stolac secondary school when Bosniak returnees returned (in the 2000–1 school year) to ensure there would be no contact between the returnees and the majority students. Rather than schools making an effort – any effort – to welcome back returnee children, there were politically motivated efforts to ensure and confirm their exclusion. Inevitably, many returnee parents voted with their feet – either deciding against return altogether, or, where the possibility existed, enrolling their children in schools outside the administrative region where the students would be 'with their own kind', despite the increased travel costs this entails (OSCE Mission to Bosnia and Herzegovina, 2007a).

The international community – including international organizations, NGOs and bilateral donors – became increasingly involved in this issue. During this phase of engagement a number of efforts were pursued in terms of supporting minimum standards for return, perhaps most importantly the *Interim Agreement on Accommodation of the Rights and Needs of Returnee Children*, signed on 5 March 2002, and aimed at stopping the most egregious instances of separation and assimilation through the introduction of a number of interim solutions.[10] This approach aimed at providing an environment in which returnee children could enjoy some limited rights to their 'own' education until the bigger political problems could be resolved. At a meeting of the Peace Implementation Council (PIC) in Brussels on 21 November 2002, the RS MoE, Federation MoE and a Deputy signed on to a series of education reform pledges.[11] A state-level Framework Law on Primary and Secondary Education was adopted in 2003, and eventually harmonized at the levels of entity, canton and Brčko District.[12] A Coordination Board to ensure implementation of the *Interim Agreement* was established, with the OSCE serving as a secretariat to keep these critical issues on the agendas of the board and the MoEs.

An increasing number of courses and activities have been promoted to teach about democracy, human rights, peacebuilding and other post-war peaceful values, and some attempt has been made to deal with the existing curricula, materials and environments. The most egregious hate speech has been removed from history textbooks, and many of the most exclusive school names and symbols removed (Donia, 2000; Karge, 2008). The concept of administrative unification of 'two schools under one roof' (2-in-1s) was adopted by some of the authorities under significant international pressure: this was supposed to be an *interim* measure (whereby children would continue to attend their classes separately, but their schools would unite to become a single institution). It was to be replaced by greater degrees of harmonization once more thorough systematic reform was achieved. The same applies to the 'Alternative National Group of Subjects' concept, or NGS, formalized under the *Interim Agreement*. Under this arrangement, returnees became able to opt out of the local curriculum for the key 'social' or 'national' subjects (language, history, geography, sometimes art or music, in addition to religious studies), while continuing to attend more neutral subjects (maths, science) together with their peers. However, both concepts, while representing an improvement, have in fact been only partly implemented, and where they are present they appear to be entrenched, rather than interim.[13]

But once education slipped from the international radar screen – replaced by concerns about police, constitutional reform issues and the broader political problems outlined above that have stalled reforms in BiH, particularly since 2006 – *systematic* reform of education stopped. As the overtly political engagement of the international community ebbed, less political approaches increasingly tried to address education reform through the side door. Roma access to education was emphasized, as this historically marginalized group has very low school attendance and completion records (OSCE Mission to Bosnia and Herzegovina, 2007b). Efforts aimed at establishing school civic bodies such as parent councils and student councils increased, with the hopes that such organizations could themselves serve as future civic voices for reform. Further, incremental long-term initiatives to lay the groundwork for less divisive and more integrative curricula began, with a focus on experts, authors and pedagogues, rather than political leaders with increasingly little interest in reform of any kind.

The notion of inclusion was emphasized, with the aim of creating open and welcoming classrooms for all children; however, this has in practice tended to focus on children with special needs or micro-minorities (the handfuls of Jews, Hungarians, Czechs etc. that make up BiH's officially recognized 17 national minorities). The inclusion of minority returnee children – students from the Bosniak. Croat or Serb constituent groups, but who now live in a place where they are in the minority – is not so often embraced, and when it is, tends to be based on individual school leadership and personalities rather than a systematic commitment to equality and inclusion.[14]

Curricular Content: What Children Learn

The curricular challenges in post-war BiH include the technical/pedagogical (overburdened curricula, emphasis on facts and memorization, reliance on teacher-centered top-down classroom approaches), as well as the issues of ethnocentric and exclusive content.[15] The critical reform needs are both method and content – what children learn as well as how – and this then defines the second most needed reform, the school environment.

The courses that cause the most concern – to the international community as well as minority returnee communities – are those most associated with identity: history, language and religion. A 1999 UNESCO study of the various curricula in place for the national group of subjects revealed a number of concerning tendencies with regard to their 'politically socializing tendencies'. In the more pro-Bosniak curriculum, the review found 'a lot of neutral and tolerable components', but noted concern over the strong views conveyed of themselves as victims of aggression and genocide, as well as an active course in military education (both these elements were subsequently discontinued). The Croat curricula contained 'several neutral and tolerable elements', but had a narrowly focused orientation towards Croatia, and ignored the other nationalities in BiH. The Serb curricula were found to 'contain a lot of desirable and tolerable units, but used Serbia as a reference point and nearly ignored the Bosniaks and Croats of the country' (Stabback, 2007: 455–6). Subsequent recommendations for curricular reform – including the recommendation of the Swiss model – have all been ignored.

In 2009 the OSCE drafted a lengthy assessment of the compulsory curricula used in the country for the national group of subjects, finding some progress, but also a number of remaining areas of concern. (Elementary education is compulsory from age five/six through to 14/15). All the curricula have improved (there are various attempts to introduce critical thinking, some more superficial than others), and to differing extents have become 'moderated' – they are not so overtly nationalist in tone. However, considerable latent nationalism remains in many cases – arguably more insidious because it often takes the form of underlying assumptions or withheld information (OSCE Mission to Bosnia and Herzegovina, 2010).

Of the three main curricula under review, the mildly pro-Bosniak (Federation) curriculum goes to the greatest lengths to be more inclusive. Its history curriculum focuses successfully on minorities and avoids a nationalist tone; however, plans are underway for including an account of the Srebrenica massacre in the history books, and it remains to be seen whether the multi-perspective methodology advocated by this curriculum will be successfully realized in the textbook accounts. The literature programme is more subtly pro-Bosniak, with a slightly heavier focus on Bosniaks than on other authors, matched by an assumption in the current textbooks to assume that all pre-Ottoman traditions are Bosniak. The literature programme in all curricula is a treasury of sacrificial patriotism:

'Your people/will die for you/under my claws/so suffer not/my tear from a dream'
(Reader for the Seventh Grade of Nine Year Primary School, 2010).

The curriculum in the Croatian language is improved over past versions, but the content suggests that while 'others' should be understood (there is very little material which would enable this goal to be accomplished), a 'love' of Croatia and Croatian culture must be rigorously inculcated. (This especially applies to the upper grades of primary school, and the literature and history programs and textbooks are particularly rich in examples.) This is not surprising, considering the heavy influence of the curriculum of neighboring Croatia on BiH's Croatian language curriculum and teaching materials. There is also a strong sense of national victimhood, with the 'Turks'[16] and the Serbs usually portrayed in negative roles, if appearing at all, both in history and in literature programs and textbooks:

'What happened to Dubrovnik in 1991? Who endangered it? Who are the evil people attacking Dubrovnik?'
(Croatian Reader for the Sixth Grade of Primary School, 2010).

The RS curriculum has also improved in terms of a slightly more modern appearance and tone, but retains not only a devout, exclusive focus on Serbia and Serbs but also a considerable sense of national victimhood (again frequently focused on the 'Turks'). It is moreover the most overtly religious of the three, with religious (Orthodox) content even appearing, albeit briefly, in the early grades of scientific instruction. As is the case in counterpart books under the Croat curriculum, religious content is drawn upon heavily for both literature and history textbooks, and is specifically associated with national loyalty. (This emerges every year most powerfully at the Feast of Saint Sava, supposed to be the 'school day' for every primary school in the Republika Srpska. Revealingly, Bosniak and Croat children are usually given the day off.) However, examples of national victimhood manifestos can also be found in the subject of Geography:

'For the freedom and creation of Republika Srpska 20,000 people died, while 830,000 Serbs have been expelled from their homes and displaced'
(Geography for the Ninth Grade of Primary School, 2005)

Of particular concern in all all three curricula, but particularly the Croat and Serb, are the conflicting signals sent by teacher guidance ostensibly promoting tolerance, followed by the presentation of arguments or suggested classroom exercises that promote one side over the other.[17] Much would ultimately depend on the good will of the teacher in using integrative class approaches and presenting material in a moderate way, and considering the poor state of teacher training in the country, this is an unlikely outcome. Moreover, the guidance suggests that understanding of modern curricular approaches on the part of curriculum developers is at best superficial, and at worst counter-productive. The method is still heavily focused on the transmission and repetition of information, rather than on exploration of facts and sources, and development of critical and analytical skills.

Overall, it is very difficult to see how a minority student (whether a National Minority or a minority returnee member of one of the Constituent Peoples) studying according to *any* of these curricula would feel truly integrated and welcomed. Moreover, the system still by and large fails to promote in its students an independent critical approach, or to provide them with any balance of opposing views. As a result, the system is not only failing – in some cases worse than failing – to promote integration; it also fails to provide students with the skills they need to help move BiH forward as citizens, voters and potential leaders.

Meaningful education reform would be possible even in the absence of more sweeping constitutional reform. Some have recommended the Swiss model, in which peoples/cantons/entities could have their own curricula while ensuring sufficient integration and core elements, the definition of 'sufficient' would probably remain the key point of contention in the absence of political will for change. (Koulouh-Westin, 2004). Stabback suggests three options. First, a common curriculum, which would be exactly what it sounds like and is politically impossible in the current situation. Second, a common core curriculum approach (which is to some extent in place, but has been hampered by the fact that 'core' was defined in a way that excludes the most important (and most controversial) elements of the National Group of Subjects). Third would be a curriculum framework with common curricular standards, to seek higher quality and modern standards, while minimizing reluctance among education authorities and politicians (Stabback, 2007: 463). However it is unclear how this might work in terms of breaking down the current ethnic flavor of school buildings. While a framework which promotes skill-based outcomes and supports methodologies enabling independent thinking would require curricula and syllabuses at lower administrative levels to be drafted accordingly, it nevertheless remains the case that without strong training for curriculum developers and teacher educators, this would go largely unimplemented.

Conclusion

> 'The pendulum in BiH remains obstinately slanted in favor of the ideologues. For the good of the country and the future prosperity of its people, the pendulum needs to swing, dramatically and quickly, towards the interests of its children' (Stabback, 2007: 463).

It is generally taken for granted in BiH today that the notion of 'BiH citizenship' – any shared sense of 'stateness' – is weak. Older generations at least have the memory of a shared life; young generations know only the history of the war and the daily divisive rhetoric from the country's politicians (RFERL, 2011; Balkan Insight, 2011). One must wonder at how a country without a citizenship can be expected to survive; examples often provided by optimistic policymakers, such as Belgium or Lebanon, do not necessarily inspire confidence in a strong and vibrant future.

Reformed curricula will never single-handedly force a love for BiH on students; the forced sentiment of 'brotherhood and unity', already discredited by the collapse of former Yugoslavia, its erstwhile proponent, would neither sell to the public nor work. However, an approach to teaching students that is based less on exclusive ideological training, and more on critical thinking and analytical skills, can at least begin to equip students to partake in democratic processes, to exist as citizens and individuals, to live in a country governed by human rights and the rule of law, and to live in a diverse Europe and a globalized society that is increasingly heterogeneous. Such an approach can demonstrate the potential for complex identity that moves beyond the narrow construction of identity that has paralyzed politics in BiH for almost two decades, and left a legacy of ethnic cleansing in its wake. Rather than seeing government as serving 'a people', students can see that it exists to serve 'the people.'

Such an approach would also demonstrate a a real commitment to the implementation of Annex 7 of the Dayton Peace Accords, in letter and spirit. It is unrealistic to think that the goals of return could ever be successful without a real effort at reintegration. And real efforts to ensure minority return would have to include development and implementation of an education system that does not separate, segregate or distinguish among majority and minority populations in a given community or school. In 2009, the European Court of

Human Rights in Strasbourg ruled that the BiH Constitution is not compliant with the European Convention on Human Rights and Fundamental Freedoms, as only Bosniaks, Croats and Serbs (not others) are eligible to serve on the BiH State Presidency or in the BiH House of Peoples.[18]

As of November 2011 BiH has failed to reform its Constitution and electoral laws to remedy this breach. One wonders what might happen when (if?) a court case if filed by a Serb family in Mostar arguing that they are denied their rights by being forced to select between Bosniak and Croat schools. The educational rights minorities – including minority returnees – could potentially spur reform aimed at breaking down institutionalized discrimination; or it could cement them forever on the basic of giving BiH a margin of appreciation reflecting the political post-war divisions of the country.

As the country simultaneously seeks to develop a democratic government based on effective powersharing, able to cope with significant social and to political reconciliation challenges, and prepare for EU membership, a number of recommendations can provide food for thought for BiH's leaders and citizens, as well as for external actors who will probably be spending and investing much money on BiH's education system. These suggestions are aimed at ensuring that the money that is spent is spent wisely, and does not avoid the deeper problems inherent in the system for the relatively 'easier' support for technical reform.

First, there is a need for a sustained commitment to reforming and modernizing the country's curricula, teaching materials and teaching methods. Such support should have at its core both an objective to reduce substantially national biases in curricular, while at the same time increasing the amount of shared content among the country's multiple curricula. Efforts are ongoing in a few quarters (notably on the part of UNICEF, Save the Children Norway and the OSCE) to address the issues of teacher training and the contents of curricula and teaching materials – particularly the crucial National Group of Subjects – in concert with the BiH Education Agency. However, these efforts have yet to be fully funded or supported. Far more attention needs to be paid to this crucial area of education reform in a post-conflict society, not only in the country but also more widely, in academic studies and in policy papers for decision-makers worldwide. The goal of such reform should be a school system that does not force parents and students to attend or select a school that 'belongs' to any one group. This would be a an obvious benefit to BiH's minority returnees, though it would also offer students from a 'majority group' in any given community an opportunity to learn in a more diverse and less exclusive manner. Schools should exist for their citizens.

Second, BiH needs a minimal form of state-level education structure that can ensure that lower-level implementing bodies are following the law, ensuring equal access to all students and meeting BiH's international obligations and human rights commitments. BiH does not necessarily need to have a single state-level MoE, though it could save money and increase efficiencies for an already small, poor country overburdened with administration. What it does need is a state-level enforcement mechanism that can serve as a body to which citizens who feel that their rights are being ignored may appeal. Ideally, if the lower level educational authorities do their job in ensuring education for all, these state-level mechanisms will never have to be tested. However, if they are not there, there is no recourse for the parent or student denied an appropriate education.

Third, as the country's politicians ponder Sejdic-Finci reform (a reform needed if the country is to move forward in the EU accession process), and in parallel with technical efforts to improve incrementally the country's educational system and curricular materials, human rights groups and advocates should explore possible judicial recourse to the systemic discrimination inherent in BiH's schools. The 'Serb in Mostar' case noted above is one such option; however, any 'non-majority' citizens in any community in BiH would be relevant. Testing the BiH system – through the BiH Human Rights Ombudsman, but also through the courts – could force recalcitrant officials to grapple finally with the inherent problems of having schools that serve only one group of citizens. Depending on the outcome within BiH, a court case might find its way down the long road to the European Court of Human Rights in Strasbourg. A host of anti-discrimination legislation could be referenced in such a case, and perhaps even the language in Annex 7, which not only allowed but in fact encouraged minority return to take place.

More broadly in terms of global IDP and refugee policies, the role of education in post-war settlements and development strategies should not be ignored. While BiH can be seen as a success in terms of its post-war property return process, the failure to promote and ensure sustainable and lasting minority return is clear. While the bricks and mortar will always be necessary to rebuild homes and schools in the wake of war, the hearts and minds aspects of education that take place inside the school building are equally, if not more, important. Political imperatives will of course always play a role between and among parties in conflict; external actors, whether peace mediators or post-war development specialists, can be prepared to set standards to be met to ensure that schools are not used to continue ethnic cleansing by peaceful means. There is some room for optimism, as education is at least increasingly on the minds of conflict resolution and development specialists, and is to be found in relevant policy papers (Bush and Saltarelli, 2000, Weinstein et al., 2009: 45). In 2011, UNESCO made explicit the link between education, peace implementation and state-building: 'Education has a central role to play in any peacebuilding and state-building enterprise, starting with the peace settlement. Peace agreements can signal that governments are setting a new course by including education in wider processes aimed at addressing, through more inclusive policies, the real and perceived injustices that underlie violent conflict' (2011: 222–3). In Sarajevo in 2009, a conference called 'Where Peace Begins' was sponsored by Save the Children, an effort notable for its emphasis on ensuring that education is included in peace talks and the fact that quality education in 'conflict-affected fragile states' must include efforts aimed at ensuring that content is oriented towards long-term stability.[19] These are small but important steps.

In 2011, education is both the cause of and potential solution to BiH's political problems, social tension and identity crisis. In BiH (and in other fragile states) education is not an optional reform that can be relegated to small humanitarian or development project implementers. It is at the core of the long-term effort to build an educated future citizenry capable of independent critical thought, and prepared for life in an increasingly diverse and globalized Europe and world. Sixteen years after the end of the war, BiH is grooming three separate groups of citizens for that future. BiH's future would undoubtedly be stronger if the country's human resources – all its citizens – would be prepared to find common solution to shared problems, through a shared vision of their potential life in Europe. Until there is political and social agreement on such an approach, neither returnees nor citizens will be able to enjoy lasting security, opportunity and peace.

Notes

1   For a thorough review of the demographic changes of the war see *Bosnia Remade: Ethnic Cleansing and its Reversal*, by Gerard Toal and Carl Dahlman, Oxford: Oxford University Press, 2011.
2   General Framework Agreement for Peace, Annex 7, Article II(5).
3   Una Sana/Bihac, Tuzla Podrinje, Zenica Doboj, Gorazde and Sarajevo.
4   Posavina, West Herzegovina, and Livno.

5   Central Bosnia and Neretva.

6   For a review of the impact of this structure on the political process in BiH, see the *Opinion on the Constitutional Situation in Bosnia and Herzegovina and the Powers of the High Representative*, adopted by the Venice Commission (European Commission for Democracy through Law), 11–12 March 2005; Foreign Policy Initiative BiH, *Governance Structures in BiH: Capacity, Ownership, EU Integration, Functioning State*, Sarajevo: Foreign Policy Initiative, 2007.

7   The national group of subjects are found in areas with high return, including Zvornik, Srebrenica, Bijeljina, Doboj, Tuzla, Prijedor, Foca and Drvar.

8   The list includes the Universal Declaration of Human Rights (1948); the Covenant on Economic, Social and Cultural Rights (1966); the Convention of the Rights of the Child (1989).

9   The OHR was established in the Dayton Agreement, Annex 10 as the main civilian capacity overseeing peace implementation (see www.ohr.int).

10 It must be noted that many of the interim solutions – most notably the two-schools-under-one roof and the national group of subjects – are still in place in 2009, as there is no will among domestic actors to change the status quo.

11 The pledges were developed through six thematic working groups in which approximately 80% of the working group members were local BiH experts. The Agenda was mainly drafted by the MoCA with input from OHR and OSCE staff. The following summarizes the highlights of each pledge: 1) Access to quality education in integrated multicultural schools; 2) Provide basic education at pre-school primary and general secondary levels with modern curriculum and systems of assessment, in well-managed and equipped schools; 3) Support BiH economic development through development of modern and flexible vocational education program; 4) Raise the quality of higher education and research in BiH; 5) Ensure transparent, equitable and cost-effective use of public resources for education.

12 Canton 10 failed to harmonize its legislation with the Framework Law on Primary and Secondary Education, so it was subsequently imposed. In Central Bosnia Canton and West Herzegovina Canton, amendments (primarily related to issues of language) to cantonal laws were imposed to ensure harmonization with the Framework Law Note cantonal

harmonization/imposition issues; Central Bosnia Canton accepted the imposed amendments, while West Herzegovina Canton did not.

13 Administratively unified 2-in-1 schools exist only in Canton 4, with the exception of Mostar Gymnasium. All other such schools continue to separate children completely, despite the mixed nature of the communities in which they live. Examples of schools offering the NGS include schools in Drvar (Canton 10) and Prijedor and Janja (RS) among others.

14 One such effort is entitled 'Index for Inclusion', from the Center for Studies on Inclusive Education (www.csie.org.uk) The Index was developed in the United Kingdom, has been translated into more than 25 languages, and is in use around the world. In BiH, the effort is being jointly implemented by Save the Children and the OSCE MBiH.

15 The concept of curricular standards or frameworks rather than thick, encyclopedic, detailed instructions – the 'nastavni plan i program', reflects the old-fashioned and prescriptive approach to teaching. Stabback notes, 'the failures of BiH syllabuses to acknowledge in any meaningful way the diversity of student learning outcomes that should be the goal of any modern syllabus- a broad range of knowledge, skills (both practical and intellectual), values and attitudes'. Stabback, Phil. 'Common curriculum, core curriculum or common curriculum standards – finding a solution of Bosnia and Herzegovina'. *Prospects*. Vol. 37, 2007, p. 451.

16 It can be recalled that 'Turks' was frequently used as a synonym for Bosniaks by Serb and Croat forces and politicians during the wartime period, and also appears in much literature now studied in schools. Both Croat and Serb textbooks regularly use this term in preference to the more correct term of 'Ottoman', when describing the Ottoman Empire.

17 See, for example, the Democracy and Human Rights curriculum for the sixth grade of Republika Srpska primary schools (unmodified since 2006). The topic is religious diversity; the method is the school celebration of Saint Sava.

18 *Case of Sejdic and Finci v. Bosnia and Herzegovina*, European Court of Human Rights, Judgment, 9; 22 December 2009, available at cmiskp.echr. coe.int/tkp197/view.asp?action=html&documentId=860268&portal=hbk m&source=externalbydocnumber&table=F69A27FD8FB86142BF01C11 66DEA398649

19 See www.savethechildren.net/alliance/what_we_do/rewritethefuture/peace/ bosnia.html for the conference report and additional information on the initiative.

References

Balkan Insight, (20 October 2011), 'Bosnian Serb Leader Blamed for Fomenting Crisis'. www. balkaninsight.com/en/article/muslim-presidency-member-accuses-rs-president (Accessed 17 December 2011).

Bassuener, K. and Weber, B. (2010), 'Are We There Yet? International Impatience vs. A Long-term Strategy for a Viable Bosnia'. *Democratization Policy Council Briefing Paper.*

Bose, Sumantra (2002), *Bosnia After Dayton: Nationalist Partition and International Intervention.* London: Hurst & Company.

Burg, Steven L. and Paul S. Shoup (2000), *The War in Bosnia –Herzegovina: Ethnic Conflict and International Intervention.* London: M. E. Sharpe.

Bush, Kenneth D. and Diana Saltarelli, (2000), *The Two Faces of Education in Ethnic Conflict: Towards a Peacebuilding Education for Children.* Florence, Italy: UNICEF.

Chivvis, Christopher (2010), 'Back to the Brink in Bosnia?', *Survival: Global Politics and Strategy.* 52 (1).

Dewey, John (1916), *Democracy and Education.* New York: The Free Press.

Donia, Robert (2000), 'The Quest for Tolerance in Sarajevo's Textbooks,' *Human Rights Review,* 1 (2).

Jansen, Stef. ' "Home" and Return in the Foreign Intervention in Bosnia and Herzegovina: An Anthropological Critique'. *Deconstructing the Reconstruction: Human Rights and the Rule of Law in post-war Bosnia and Herzegovina.* Dina Francesca Hayes (ed.), Hampshire: Ashgate, 2008, pp. 29–51,

Karge, Heike (2008), '20th Century History in the Textbooks of Bosnia and Herzegovina: An Analysis of Books used for the Final Grades of Primary School'. Braunschweig, Germany: Georg Eckert Institute for International Textbook Research.

McMahon, Patrice C. and Jon Western (September – October 2009), 'The Death of Dayton: How to Stop Bosnia from Falling Apart'. *Foreign Affairs.*

Mooney, Erin. (18–19 June 2008), 'Securing Durable Solutions for Displaced Persons in Georgia: The Experience in Bosnia and Herzegovina'. Paper presented at conference, *Conflict and Migration: The Georgian-Abkhazian Case in A European Context.* Istanbul.

OSCE Mission to Bosnia and Herzegovina (2007a), *Tailoring Catchment Areas.* www.oscebih.org/ documents/osce_bih_doc_2007102409165004eng.pdf (Accessed 17 September 2011).

—(2007b), *Slipping through the Cracks: School Enrolment and Completion in Bosnia and Herzegovina: A Status Report.* www.oscebih.org (Accessed 17 September 2011).

—(2007c), *Lessons from Education Reform in Brčko.* www.oscebih.org (Accessed 17 September 2011).

—(2010), *Analysis of the National Group of Subjects in the Compulsory Curricula of Bosnia and Herzegovina.*

Perry, Valery (2006), 'Democratic Ends, (un)Democratic Means? Reflections on Democratization Strategies in Brcko and Bosnia-Herzegovina'. *Bosnian Security After Dayton: New Perspectives.* Michael Innes (ed.). Routledge.

Phuong, Catherine (2000), ' "Freely to Return": Reversing Ethnic Cleansing in Bosnia-Herzegovina'. *Journal of Refugee Studies,* 13 (2).

RFERL (2011), 'Bosnia's Escalating War of Words'. www.rferl.org/content/bosnia_escalating_war_of_words/24364968.html (Accessed 10 January 2012).

Stabback, Phil (2007), 'Common curriculum, core curriculum or common curriculum standards – finding a solution of Bosnia and Herzegovina'. *Prospects.* Vol. 37.

Stefansson, Anders (2008), 'Urban Exile: Locals, Newcomers and the Cultural Transformation of Sarajevo'. *The New Bosnian Mosaic: Identifies, Memories and Moral Claims in a Post-War Society.* Xavier Bougarel, Elissa Helms, and Ger Duijzings (Eds). Hampshire, English: Ashgate.

UNESCO (2011), Education for All Global Monitoring report, *The Hidden Crisis: Armed Conflict and Education.* Paris: UNESCO.

Weinstein, Harvey M., Sarah Warshauer Freedman and Holly Hughson (2009) 'School Voices: Challenges Facing Education Systems After Identity-Based Conflicts', in *Education, Citizenship and Social Justice*, 2 (1).

Challenges for the International Aid System

Alan Smith

8

Abstract

This chapter identifies a number of significant developments in the global environment that have influenced international aid over the past decade and reflects on their implications for the provision of education for IDPs. These include arguments for the inclusion of education as part of a humanitarian response, changes to the global security environment, and the implications of UN involvement in peacebuilding. It argues that there is a lack of understanding around the roles education may play in the wake of crisis, as well as the contexts in which people are internally displaced.

Introduction

When the cold war ended, there was an aspiration that the international aid agenda might be driven by humanitarian goals to eliminate poverty rather than be limited by tensions in international relations. This aspiration is reflected in the Millennium Development Goals (MDGs) and the central importance of education to human development was emphasized by the identification of six Education for All (EFA) goals to be achieved by the year 2015. Since these goals were agreed at a meeting in Dakar in 2000, progress has been monitored by the EFA Global Monitoring Report (GMR), produced annually by an independent team and published by UNESCO. The 2011 GMR indicates that globally the number of children out of school has been reduced (from 119 million in 1998 to 67 million in 2008), although progress is too slow to meet the EFA goals by 2015. Retention of children in school is also a significant problem, for example, in sub-Saharan Africa, where ten million children drop out of school every year and another 1.9 million teachers will be needed by 2015 to achieve universal primary education.

The GMR provides some indication of the scale of the challenge of providing education for the children of internally displaced persons (IDPs), although figures for displaced persons should be treated with caution. It is difficult to estimate how many children of IDPs are out of school, but using estimates from the United Nations High Commissioner for Refugees (UNHCR) and the Internal Displacement Monitoring Centre (IDMC) the report estimates the number of IDPs in 2009 to be 27.1 million, almost twice the number of 15.2 million refugees (GMR, 2011: 153). The highest concentrations of IDPs are in six countries (Sudan, Colombia, Iraq, DRC, Somalia and Pakistan). Conservative estimates are that 45% of all displaced persons (refugees, IDPs and asylum seekers) are under 18 years of age (UNHCR, 2010). As highlighted in previous chapters, because of differences in definition and the legal standing of refugees and IDPs, this means that national governments have a responsibility to provide education for IDP children, but the practical reality is that this role often falls to international agencies. While barriers to education for IDPs are many, two main causes of displacement feature prominently in the literature: natural disasters and conflict. The following sections highlight how these underlying causes of displacement have become conflated within the international aid system and why the distinction is important for the provision of education for children of IDPs. In broad terms they relate to arguments that education should be part of front-line humanitarian response; increasing concerns that aid to education has become increasingly skewed by the global security agenda since 9/11; and emerging implications of education having a more prominent role in UN peacebuilding.

Education as a Humanitarian Response

For more than a decade arguments for the inclusion of education as part of a humanitarian response have strengthened for a number of reasons. One impetus was frustration among a number of NGOs and relief agencies that education was rarely included in the discourse about humanitarian response (Retamal and Aedo-Richmond, 1998) and this has meant that in emergencies, especially those that have lasted over long periods of time, children have often missed out on their right to education. The absence of education from the humanitarian discourse was highlighted by its omission from the SPHERE project, established in 1997, which became widely recognized as defining minimum standards to ensure quality and accountability of humanitarian work[1]. Resistance to the recognition of education as part of humanitarian response to emergencies has largely been to do with arguments that it is not as urgent or life-saving as emergency relief related to food, water, shelter and health. Recent figures suggest that these arguments still prevail; for example, despite a decade of advocacy, education still receives only 2% of humanitarian aid and receives the lowest response to funds requested when compared to food, health, shelter, water and sanitation (UNESCO, 2011). Despite this, the field has developed significantly since the World Education Forum in 2000 and the argument for education is not so much that it is more important than these other factors, but that education is often neglected, and there is increasing recognition that education is an important factor in the physical, psychosocial and cognitive protection of children during emergencies. By providing a sense of stability, education may ease the psychosocial impacts. A safe learning environment may shield them from the everyday physical violence. Education can also provide cognitive protection by supporting intellectual development through the teaching of literacy and numeracy, while also conveying life-saving information on how to protect oneself from danger[2].

The Dakar Framework for Action included an explicit call for donor support to the field now known as education in emergencies and an important initiative was the formation of the Inter-Agency Network on Education in Emergencies (INEE) led by UNESCO, UNHCR, UNICEF, Norwegian Refugee Council, CARE International and the Save the Children Alliance. INEE does not have the mandate to implement or coordinate during crises, but enables members to share information and encourages collaboration. An important goal for INEE has been to define minimum standards for education in emergencies and these standards are currently being used in over 60 countries. Additionally, the UNESCO Institute for Educational Planning (IIEP) has provided research, training and publications with a focus on education in emergencies and reconstruction. One of the most significant contributions to the early work was a global survey of education in emergencies that documented how many refugee, displaced and returnee children and young people had access to education and the nature of the education they received (Women's Commission for Refugee Women and Children, 2004). It documented how in 2002 more than 27 million children and young people affected by armed conflict, including refugees and internally displaced persons (IDPs), did not have access to formal education, and that the vast majority of these (more than 90%) were internally displaced or within their country of origin. Of these, adolescents and young people had the least access to formal education, and country case studies highlighted the high value that displaced families place on access to education. The report also documented practical challenges for education in emergencies in terms of overcrowded classrooms, lack of qualified teachers with little or no compensation, lack of certification and recognition of students' learning and risks for girls related to sexual exploitation.

INEE has since grown significantly and now has more than 6,000 members from a variety of organizations. Over the years it has developed a toolkit that contains 'a wide variety of practical, field-friendly tools and resources to guide educationalists, humanitarian workers and government officials working in the field of education in emergencies through to recovery' (INEE, 2012). As well as the Minimum Standards, guidance notes have been developed in various languages on 'Safer School Construction', 'Teacher Compensation', 'Teaching and Learning', 'Inclusive Education' and 'Gender', as well as a reference guide to 'External Education Funding'.

One challenge for such a network is that it brings together people and agencies working in emergencies that are generated by very diverse causes. It could also be argued that the inclusion of so many different contexts within the broader concept of 'education and emergencies' can be confusing. It will become increasingly important to distinguish between emergencies created by humanitarian or natural disasters such as famine, health epidemics, earthquakes, floods or tsunamis and crises generated by human conflict. This is particularly important in the case of displacement of populations due to violence, since immediate responses to their predicament will be affected by the pervading political environment, and longer-term solutions will ultimately involve addressing underlying causes of conflict itself. Since the establishment of INEE there has been an increasing emphasis on conflict as one of the most significant challenges for education in emergencies and this has been emphasised by the fact that 28 million children live in conflict-affected countries, which represents 42% of the world total of children out of school (UNESCO, 2011).

Implications of a Changing Global Security Environment for the Education of IDPs

Although the number of armed conflicts in the world has declined (from fifty-four in 1990 to thirty-six in 2009), the nature of conflict is changing, with important consequences for populations and their education. After the end of the cold war, conflicts became overwhelmingly fought within rather than between states and many involve protracted violence – the average duration of conflict in low-income countries is twelve years (UNESCO, 2011). Research found that the demographic factor most closely associated with an outbreak of civil conflict during the 1990s was a high proportion of young adults (aged 15 to 29 years), and that countries in which young adults comprised more than 40% of the adult population were more than twice as likely to have an outbreak of civil conflict (Cincotta et al., 2003). Later research suggests that for every one per cent increase in a country's youth population, there is a seven per cent increase in the likelihood of civil war, and that the three determinants that made people more likely to engage in political violence were: being young, being uneducated and being without dependents (Collier, 2007). This has led to much debate about 'youth bulges' in a population, and recent studies (Curtain, 2007; Barakat and Urdal, 2009) suggest that the combination of a large youth bulge and an absence of opportunity are primary drivers of destabilization, which is particularly important since young people often represent a significant proportion of IDPs who are dislocated from their family without access to education or employment.

While the 1990s saw a change to the dynamics of violent conflict, without doubt the defining moment of the past decade was the events of 9/11 and the subsequent impact it has had in bringing global security to the top of the international development agenda (World Development Report, 2011). The changing priorities are reflected in a series of DFID working papers that considered various definitions of the concept of 'fragile states' and adopted a working definition of difficult environments as '*those areas where the state is unable or unwilling to harness domestic and international resources effectively for poverty reduction*'. These arise across a range of situations including state collapse, loss of territorial control, low administrative capacity, political instability, neo-patrimonial politics, conflict and repressive polities.[3] A second paper examined the importance of working in 'difficult environments' in achieving the Millennium Development Goals (MDGs) and by developing a proxy list of 46 countries, concluded that '*a third of people living in absolute poverty around the world, live in difficult environments*'.[4] A third paper examined ways of improving the provision of social services in difficult environments as a central task for poverty reduction and identified a range of promising approaches including, strengthening pro-poor policy-making (for example, by strengthening state capacity including use of non-state mechanisms); by building capacity of state- and non-state providers; and by reducing barriers to poor people's access and participation (such as strengthening the voices of the poor and moving resources to community level). Education is identified as a crucial entry point for such an approach.[5] These working papers clearly informed the DFID Policy Paper, *Why we need to work more effectively in fragile states*, released in January 2005. However, by then the language of working in difficult environments had disappeared but the policy paper committed DFID to give greater priority to working with 'fragile states' through a commitment to review the way in which aid is allocated and to work with partners over more realistic five–ten year timeframes.

Significantly, USAID also produced a strategy paper in January 2005 that identified development as the 'third pillar' of US foreign policy on a par with 'defence' and 'diplomacy':

> 'The strategy recognises that a root of the national security threat to the United States and the broader international community is the lack of development, which can't be addressed by military or diplomatic means alone. In countries that lack the ability, or will, to provide basic services or protection, we can no longer choose to look the other way. We need to engage in a coordinated and strategic manner to address the core issues of poverty and underdevelopment.'
>
> (USAID, 2005)

This seems to be the period when many of the major international development agencies, including AusAID, CIDA, DFID, the Netherlands Ministry of Foreign Affairs and USAID, developed a new policy related to international development assistance known as the 3D approach (Diplomacy, Defence and

Development) which seeks to integrate and embed development assistance within national diplomatic and security priorities. This institutionalized the view, particularly post 9/11, that development failures in low-income countries have direct security implications for industrialized countries. This has resulted in increased funding to conflict-affected countries, particularly those of strategic political importance: coupled with the general increase in ODA, aid to these states nearly tripled in real terms between 2000 and 2006 and in 2006 Iraq and Afghanistan accounted for over 60% of all aid to conflict-affected countries (Novelli, 2001: 4).

The implications for the provision of education have been significant and are reflected in the GMR in a number of ways. First, the report highlights concerns about links between aid and security. It identifies twenty-one developing countries that are spending more on arms and the military than on primary schools and presents evidence that the amount of aid to certain countries may be driven more by global security concerns rather than poverty and need. It highlights the use of education to 'win hearts and minds' as part of counterinsurgency strategy in Iraq and Afghanistan and raises concerns about the confusion of roles between military and aid personnel.

Secondly, the GMR highlights how most violence in conflict-affected countries is directed towards civilians and mass displacement is one of the main consequences (GMR, 2011: 137). The use of violence against civilians as a weapon of war adds additional dangers and complexities in attempting to make education provision for IDPs. This is further illustrated by reports of an increasing number of attacks on education that use political and military violence against education staff, students, teachers unions, government officials and institutions. A global study (O'Malley, 2010) found intentional attacks in at least 31 countries between 2007 and 2009. A recent development has been the formation of a Global Coalition to Protect Education from Attack (GCPEA) and UNESCO has produced a report on 'Protecting Education from Attack' that explores possible motives, responses and prevention strategies including armed protection, community defense and strengthening international monitoring systems. GCPEA is currently establishing a knowledge base by documenting the number and range of attacks. To date these include a global study as well as a number of country case studies.[6]

Increasing Involvement of the UN in Peacebuilding

Another significant development over the past decade has been an increasing commitment of the UN to peacebuilding and this too has implications for the extent to which UN organizations, rather than national governments, are likely to become more involved in making education provision for IDPs. Since its establishment the UN has been concerned with peacekeeping through monitoring of ceasefires, verifying troop withdrawals, patrolling borders and demilitarized zones. By the late 1990s, however, the notion of an 'integrated mission' was developed to ensure a system-wide UN response to the challenges of improving coordination, reducing duplication and providing a means for all UN actors at the country level to work together towards achieving a common objective. The concept of 'peacebuilding' received renewed attention following the UN Secretary General's call for the establishment of the Peacebuilding Commission (PBC), the Peacebuilding Support Office (PBSO) and the Peacebuilding Fund (PBF) in 2006. These structures emerged because of concerns to prevent relapses in the aftermath of conflict. They provide support to countries in the immediate post-conflict period mainly through funding for political, governance, security and macro-economic reforms (Smith, McCandless, Paulson and Wheaton, 2010).

In 2010 the PBF had funds of US$360 million and was supporting more than 150 projects in 18 countries, but social programming, such as education, had received less than 14% of its funds. The PBF mission is to 'address immediate needs in countries emerging from conflict at a time when sufficient resources are not available from other funding mechanisms and to support interventions of direct and immediate relevance to the peacebuilding process'.[7] It further states that 'the use of PBF resources is meant to catalyze and encourage longer-term engagements by development agencies and bilateral donors'. The UN Peacebuilding Fund (PBF) has limitations. It only has a funding window of 2–3 years in the immediate post-conflict period and the priority areas funded to date have been related to macro reforms with priority for security, political and economic sector reforms. There have been criticisms of this approach. For example, Collier and Hoeffler (2002) concluded that focusing on social policies such as education and healthcare, as opposed to macroeconomic reforms, is especially important for preserving peace in countries that have emerged from civil conflict. Paris (2004) also highlights the limitations and sometimes negative effects of peacebuilding that focuses exclusively on electoral and economic reforms that tend to address the concerns of political elites and powerful groups rather than provide more immediate 'peace dividends' for marginalized groups and local communities. Yet durable solutions are a central part of peacebuilding; for example, the UN Security Council has also recognized the destabilizing effect of displacement and threat to sustainable peace: 'Unresolved problems of displacement may cause instability, engender new, or renew, conflicts, and thus threaten peace processes and peacebuilding efforts. As such, durable solutions are a central concern for the Security Council.' (Security Council, Internal Displacement and Protection: p. 38, Brookings Institution); and the UN General Assembly notes that 'durable solutions for internally displaced persons, including through voluntary return, sustainable reintegration and rehabilitation processes and their active participation, as appropriate, in the peace process are necessary elements of effective peacebuilding' (A/RES/62/153 (2008) on Protection of and Assistance to Internally Displaced Persons, paragraph 8).

With regard to the UN peacebuilding architecture, the General Assembly 'welcomes the role of the Peacebuilding Commission in this regard, and continues to urge the Commission to intensify its efforts, within its mandate, in cooperation with national and transitional Governments and in consultation with the relevant United Nations entities, to incorporate the rights and the specific needs of internally displaced persons, including their voluntary return in safety and with dignity, reintegration and rehabilitation, as well as related land and property issues, when advising on or proposing country-specific peacebuilding strategies for post-conflict situations in cases under consideration' (A/RES/64/162 (2010) on Protection of and Assistance to Internally Displaced Persons, paragraph 9.)

The PBF provides an opportunity to bridge the gap between emergency humanitarian response and peacebuilding since its remit includes the possibility of 'seeding' longer term processes necessary for sustainable peace. OECD/DAC principles suggest that early and sustained engagement is crucial in conflict-affected contexts. Opportunities therefore exist for the PBF to fund education programming that identifies, anticipates and initiates longer-term peacebuilding needs, particularly in areas such as education provision for IDPs where national governments find it difficult to access funding and displaced youth populations provide a threat to future stability.

Conclusion

At first glance there appears to be a tension in the developments which have influenced international aid and education programming over the past decade. On the one hand there has been a move to include education as part of 'neutral' humanitarian response. On the other hand, the merging of security and development agendas has seen increasing recognition of the political environment in which educationalists are situated and with which they must engage. However, what appears as a conflict is in reality a failure to delineate the different roles education has to play in different contexts.

One role for education in the wake of crisis is in helping to provide a 'return to normality'. As previous chapters have demonstrated this is particularly relevant following natural disaster. While there are 'windows of opportunity' in rebuilding post-disaster, there should be a limit to the degree of experimentation, at least with short-term humanitarian funding. Certainly in the case of the sector response to Hurricane Katrina, a patchwork of policies designed to 'fix' the education system left displaced students with relatively few options and increased disruption to their family life and support networks.

In contrast, analysis of conflict-affected societies demonstrates the problems 'normality' may have caused in the lead up to the war. Systematic analysis of education systems from a conflict perspective is still an underdeveloped area. There are many entry points to the various levels of an education system. These include a critical analysis of the political ideology driving a system, as well as its legislative, structural and administrative features. These may have implications for non-discrimination and equal access to education. Areas of the curriculum related to identity are sometimes referred to as 'national subjects', in many instances tightly controlled by governments and regarded as essential tools for nation building. The choice of language of instruction confers a power and prestige through its use in formal instruction. Not only is there a symbolic aspect, referring to status and visibility, but also a conceptual aspect referring to shared values and worldview expressed through and in that language. While from a practical perspective some aid workers have expressed concerns that this type of critical analysis may make it more difficult to maintain positive relationships with local education officials, in contested societies these are all areas which require serious thought.

Indeed, it is becoming increasingly clear that it is difficult to work effectively in the highly politicized context of conflict without engaging in the process of peacebuilding. The role education can play in these processes may range from a curriculum designed to promote social cohesion, to its role in underpinning wider societal transformation with human rights values and commitment to non-violence. It is however conceptually confusing to include this type of education programming under the label 'education in emergencies' as it suggests a more political and interventionist stance. It also causes frustrations in terms of funding. These are long-term processes and require long-term predictable, rather than short-term humanitarian, financing.

Adding to the confusion is the conflation of contexts within the term 'internal displacement'. The conditions leading to internal displacement are broad; the definition included in the Guiding Principles extends beyond those forced to flee due to conflict and persecution to include those displaced due to natural and human-made disaster. This is because displaced persons share distinct protection and assistance needs arising from the involuntary nature of their movement. IDPs certainly face a number of common barriers in accessing their right to education and serious thought should be given in any context to difficulties surrounding documentation, insecurity and discrimination. However, a common definition ceases to be useful when it masks differences in context. This book has made an important contribution to our understanding of the roles education plays in different contexts of displacement. In the context of increasing internal displacement there is a pressing need for education planners to make explicit their theories of change and to take context as the starting point for programming.

Notes

1 www.sphereproject.org/about/

2 www.ineesite.org/post/about_education_in_emergencies1/

3 PRDE Working Paper 1 (Aug 2004), *Fragile States: Defining Difficult Environments for Poverty Reduction*, Poverty Reduction in Difficult Environments Team, Policy Division, DFID www.oecd.org/dataoecd/30/62/34041714.pdf

4 PRDE Working Paper 2 (Sept 2004) *How Important Are Difficult Environments to Achieving the MDGs?*, Poverty Reduction in Difficult Environments Team, Policy Division, DFID www.oecd.org/dataoecd/30/63/34041723.pdf

5 PRDE Working Paper 3 (Oct 2004), *Approaches to Improving the Delivery of Social Services in Difficult Environments*, Poverty Reduction in Difficult Environments Team, Policy Division, DFID www.oecd.org/dataoecd/31/0/34041738.pdf

6 www.protectingeducation.org

7 www.unpbf.org/mission.shtml

References

Barakat and Urdal (2009), World Bank Working Paper, 'Breaking the Waves: Does education mediate the relationship between youth bulges and political violence'. Washington, DC: The World Bank.

Collier, P. (2007), *The Bottom Billion: Why the Poorest Countries Are Failing and What Can Be Done About It*. New York: Oxford University Press.

Curtain, R. (2007), 'For Poor Countries' Youth, Dashed Hopes Signal Danger Ahead'. *Current History* (105) 695.

IDMC (2011), *Internal Displacement: Global Overview of Trends and Developments in 2010*. Geneva: IDMC.

Novelli, M. (2010), 'The New Geopolitics of Educational Aid: From Cold Wars to Holy Wars?' *International Journal of Educational Development* 30, 5.

O'Malley, B. (2010a), *Education Under Attack 2010*. Paris: UNESCO.

—(2010b), *The Longer Term Impact of Attacks on Education on Education Systems, Development and Fragility and the Implications for Policy Responses*. Background paper for EFA Global Monitoring Report 2011.

Retamal, G. and Aedo-Richmond, R. (eds) (1998), *Education as a Humanitarian Response*. Cassell: London.

Smith, A. (2010), The influence of education on conflict and peace building, Background paper prepared for the *Education for All Global Monitoring Report 2011 The Hidden Crisis: Armed conflict and education*, Paris: UNESCO.

UK Department for International Development (2005), *Policy Paper: Why we need to work more effectively in fragile states*. London: DFID.

UNESCO (2010), *Protecting Education From Attack*. Paris: UNESCO.

—(2011), *Education For All Global Monitoring Report 2011. The hidden crisis: Armed conflict and education*. Paris: UNESCO.

UNHCR (2010), *Global Trends: Refugees 2009 Global Trends: Refugees, Asylum-Seekers, Returnees, Internally Displaced and Stateless Persons*. Geneva: United Nations High Commissioner for Refugees.

USAID (2005), *Fragile States Strategy*, US Agency for International Development. Washington, DC: US Department for International Development.

Women's Commission for Refugee Women and Children (2004), *Global Survey on Education in Emergencies*. New York: Women's Commission for Refugee Women and Children.

World Bank (2011), *World Development Report 2011: Conflict, Security and Development*. Washington: The World Bank.

Index